365 DAYS

365
DAYS

Ronald J. Glasser

George Braziller

NEW YORK

TO THE MEMORY OF

Stephen Crane

First published in 1971 by George Braziller, Inc.

Copyright © 1971, 2003 by Ronald J. Glasser

For information, please address the publisher:
George Braziller, Inc.
171 Madison Avenue
New York, New York 10016

Library of Congress Cataloging-in-Publication Data:
Glasser, Ronald J.
    365 days / Ronald J. Glasser.—2nd ed.
    p. cm.
    ISBN 0-8076-1527-7 (pbk.)
    1. Vietnamese Conflict, 1961–1975. I. Title: Three hundred
sixty-five days. II. Title.
DS557.7.G54 2004
959.704'3'0922—dc22   2003063579

Printed and bound in the United States of America

Second edition

Contents

Preface to the Second Edition   VII

Preface to the First Edition   IX

1. Go Home, Kurt   5
2. Mayfield   31
3. Medics   49
4. Final Pathological Diagnosis   57
5. The Shaping-Up of McCabe   63
6. Search and Destroy   93
7. Come On! Let's Go!   107
8. No Fucken Cornflakes   113
9. Track Unit   127
10. Gentlemen, It Works   149
11. Bosum   181
12. Me Either   191
13. Choppers   195
14. Joan   209
15. $90,000,000 a Day   227
16. Brock   239
17. I Don't Want to Go Home Alone   257

Glossary of Military and Medical Terms   289

Preface to the Second Edition

I WROTE *365 Days* in the midst of the Vietnam War. The book was completely finished before I left Asia for the States. What editing there was amounted to no more than shifting around some of the chapters and ending the occasional paragraph a sentence or two earlier. There was no need to change much else—it was simply the truth as it stood. What strikes me today, three decades later, is how well the stories have maintained their power, how few of those kids we were able to completely mend, and how, after all these years, so many are still dead.

Today we are in the midst of a new war in Iraq. The heat, the confusion, the shock are all like Nam. What is different is the nature of the wounds and how many die. In Vietnam, if you made it to a chopper, you'd probably survive. Not in Iraq. The body armor of this new army is very good. The penetrating chest wounds, the ruptured aortas, the shattered livers and spleens, the collapsed lungs, and the massive internal hemorrhages so common in the Mekong Delta and up along the Cambodian border are part of that other war. But the number of troopers with head wounds, those who are blind, who come off the choppers with no hands or arms, with their legs crushed or blown off—injuries common in Iraq—were not seen at the military hospitals in Da Nang or Cu Chi. The terribly wounded in Nam usually never made it to the hospitals.

In Vietnam it was rare to be killed flat-out—one moment

alive and the next dead. It happened, but it was the exception, and it was for the most part unexpected, the result of a lucky shot or a booby trap. In Iraq, they are right up close to you. No body armor, no matter how good, can protect against an RPG fired from a nearby street corner five meters away, nor can a trooper survive when, standing in line to buy a Coke from a sidewalk vendor, someone walks up from behind and shoots him in the head. When you die in Iraq, you die right there. There is little chance of being alive when the med evac lands if someone walking past a Humvee casually drops a hand grenade into the backseat, or if they let tanks and armored personal carriers pass during an ambush, only to detonate a buried roadside 105-mm shell under a thin-skinned half-ton truck or Humvee. There is none of the haphazardness of Vietnam. In Nam, fate gave you a chance. In Iraq, they are close enough to touch you when you die.

When I wrote these stories, they were a way of making sure that the unimaginable bravery and courage I witnessed in Vietnam would not be forgotten and that what the war really meant would not be lost forever to those who had fought it nor remain a mystery to their families. If there was a lesson in the experiences of Vietnam, or if there was to be any sense of redemption, I was convinced it could come only from the recounting of the individual acts of those who had paid the price.

At the beginning of the twenty-first century, the stories in *365 Days* will perhaps find a new resonance by teaching us what happens when wars are started for no clear-cut reason, when battles are joined without the slightest understanding of the real consequences, and when, once again, conflicts are concocted by men who have little, if any, interest or concern for those they put in harm's way.

Preface to the First Edition

THESE pages were not written in desperation, nor were they written out of boredom, nor even, I think, to prove a point, but rather to offset the sinking feeling we all had that someday, when the whole thing was over, there would be nothing remembered except the confusion and the politics.

There is, of course, something else to be remembered.

There was a time the Army hospitals in Japan were averaging six to eight thousand patients a month. (During the Tet offensive it had been closer to eleven.) I was assigned to one of these hospitals, and I remember days and sometimes weeks when the choppers never stopped coming in. When they couldn't fly, the Army brought the casualties overland from the Air Force bases in ambulance buses. The surgeons and even the internists seemed ready for the emergency. But I had been sent to Japan as a pediatrician to serve the children of the dependent military population there.

I soon realized that the troopers they were pulling off those med evac choppers were only children themselves.

Loss is a part of pediatrics. Two infants in four thousand are born with a severe congenital anomaly; fifteen percent of all prematures are mentally retarded; one out of twenty thousand children will get leukemia. The rest you struggle over: the meningitises, the pneumonias, the poisonings, and the accidents. They set the tone, for to save one child is to save the whole thing.

But to save him only to see him blown apart or blinded, to help him grow properly only to have his spinal cord transected or to have him burned to death, puts all the effort in doubt; the vaccines, the pediatric research, the new techniques and the endless concern—suddenly it all seemed so foolish, so hopeless. To lose a child, at any time along his life, is really to lose the whole thing.

Zama, where I was assigned in September 1968, was a 700-bed hospital with a small pediatric unit of five beds and a nursery. It was the only general Army hospital in Japan. There were internists, anesthesiologists, ophthalmologists, obstetricians, gynecologists, oral surgeons, dermatologists, plastic surgeons, ENT specialists, thoracic surgeons, vascular surgeons, and even an allergist.

It was an excellent hospital. There is not, I think, a community in America that would not have been proud and happy to have had our hospital, just as it was, serving it. Literally thousands of boys were saved. But the effort had its price; after a while it all began to seem so natural, even the blind seventeen-year-olds stumbling down the hallway, or the shattered high-school football player being wheeled to physical therapy. I can remember stepping out of the pediatric clinic into a corridor filled with forty to fifty litter cases, walking past them and joking where I could, but not feeling particularly involved. At first, when it was all new, I was glad I didn't know them; I was relieved they were your children, not mine. After a while, I changed. These kids were so brave, they endured so much, they were so uncomplaining that you couldn't help but feel proud of them. I can remember only one boy who would not stop screaming.

In the beginning I talked to the kids just to have something to say and to get them talking. Later I came to realize they were all saying the same things—without quite saying them. They were worried, every one of them, not about the big things, not about survival, but about how they would explain away their lost legs or the weakness in their right arms. Would they embarrass their families? Would they be able to make it at parties where guys were still whole? Could they go to the beach, and would their scars darken in the sun and offend the girls? Would they be able to get special cars? Above all, and underlining all their cares, would anybody love them when they got back? I would leave the head wounds with the frightening thought that someday someone might ask them what had happened to their faces.

The stories I have tried to tell here are true. Those that happened in Japan I was part of; the rest are from the boys I met. I would have liked to have disbelieved some of them, and at first I did, but I was there long enough to hear the same stories again and again, and then to see part of it myself.

Initially, there was no thought of putting these sketches on paper, for that is what they are—sketches, not finished stories. I did not start writing for months, and even then it was only to tell what I was seeing and being told, maybe to give something to these kids that was all theirs without doctrine or polemics, something they could use to explain what they might not be able to explain themselves. It was a brutal time for them, and in fairness I have changed the names, dates, deployments, and some unit designations.

I certainly did not see it all, and in truth I have dealt with only a small part, but I saw enough, more than enough. They all came through Japan: the 9th Division fighting in the Delta—the Riverines—the 1st Air Cav, the 101st, the 4th and the 25th, the 1st and the 173rd, the chopper pilots and the RTO's, the forward observers, the cooks, the medics and the sergeants, the colonels and the contractors, the Special-Forces troopers and the Rangers, the heroes and the ones under military arrest, the drug addicts and the killers. Sooner or later they all came to us at Zama.

If there is more to say, it will have to be said by others, though I wonder how they will do it. There is no novel in Nam: there is not enough for a plot, nor is there really any character development. If you survive 365 days without getting killed or wounded, you simply go home and take up again where you left off. And then again, it is not one war but four or five. To fight in the Delta is as different from fighting in the Central Highlands as fighting in Burma was from fighting in France. The DMZ, Cambodia, Laos, North Vietnam—none of them is the same.

As for me, my wish is not that I had never been in the Army, but that this book could never have been written.

R. J. G.

365 DAYS

Tonight I'm with myself again
I'm talking with my mind
These last three months we've talked a lot
And found we're in a bind

Not that we're different
We don't think we're unique
But the answers we're questioning
Are those we've heard you speak

We haven't decided you're wrong
For experience has a function
But my mind is at the crossroad
And I think I'm at a junction

You sent us here to join you
And to fight your distant war
We did, but even those who make it home
Carry back a scar

The answer that we question most
Is one we've heard you say,
"You owe it to your country, boy,
It's the American Way"

We haven't decided you're really wrong
For experience has its function
But my mind is at the crossroad
And I can't find the junction

We haven't decided you're wrong
For experience has its function
But you've thrown us out here on the backroads
And we're gonna find the junction

Ace Evers
Wounded medic
U.S. Army Hospital, Zama, Japan

1

Go Home, Kurt

WHY write anything?" Peterson said. "Who wants to be reminded?"

There are no veterans' clubs for this war, no unit reunions, no pictures on the walls. For those who haven't been there, or are too old to go, it's as if it doesn't count. For those who've been there, and managed to get out, it's like it never happened. Only the eighteen-, nineteen-, and twenty-year-olds have to worry, and since no one listens to them, it doesn't matter.

But there were 6000 patients evac'ed to Japan last month. You'd think that so many wounded would be hard to ignore, but somehow, as Peterson says, they are. They're written off each month—a wastage rate—a series of contrapuntal numbers, which seems to make it all not only acceptable, but strangely palatable as well.

Perhaps Peterson's right. And if he is, then everything is a bit closer to what Herbert said when he woke up in the recovery room and found they'd taken off his leg: "Fuck you—fuck you one and all."

Herbert lost his leg in Vietnam, but it was cut off here in Japan in the middle of the Kanto Plains. We remove a lot of limbs during all the seasons. This makes living here difficult, even without the factories. At one time these plains must have been a good place to be. There are woodblocks from the Mejii era that show it tranquil and lovely, nestled comfortably at the foot of the mountains. There is no beauty here now. Like the wounds, the rivers run, polluted and ugly, from a dirty green to a metallic gray; the rice and barley fields that used to be here have been replaced by square, filthy factories. Even the air stinks; every day is like living behind a Mexican bus. Still, no

5

one is shooting at you here. There are no ambushes or hunter-killer teams.

No one sends out the LRRP's, and at night you can't hear them pounding in mortar tubes across the paddies. That's something. You can see it on the faces of the troopers they carry in off the choppers. It doesn't matter to them that the place smells or that the smoke from Yokahama and Yokuska blots out the stars. All that counts is that their war is over for a while and this time they got out alive.

We have four Army hospitals scattered about the plains—Drake, Ojiie, Kishine, and Zama. It's hard to know what they've told you about Tet, but over here, the operating rooms never stopped. The internists and obstetricians did minor surgery, and the surgeons lived in the OR. But even when there are no offensives we're busy. We don't just get the Herberts—we get them all: the burns, the head wounds, the cords, the tumors. Medicine is always busy, too. The medical wards are full of patients with hepatitis, malaria, pneumonia, and kidney failure. It is something of an achievement that we're able to do so much. In 1966 there was only one 90-bed Army dispensary in Japan; in fact, there was little else in the rest of Asia. When President Johnson chose to listen to his military advisers and send in ground troops, the Army had the choice of expanding the existing medical facilities here in Japan, building up those in the Philippines, or starting from scratch in Okinawa. Okinawa was too expensive—something about cost plus and American-type labor unions. The Philippines looked a bit too unstable, and so, despite Okinawa being four hours closer to Nam,

6

and the Philippines having more available land, the Army chose Japan.

Everything was put here into the Kanto Plains and clustered around the Air Force bases at Tachikawa and Yokota. The Air Force brings our patients in over the mountains in their C-141's. They stay at Yokota overnight at the 20th casualty staging area, where they're stabilized. A lot of them have already been operated on before they arrive— some massively—and it's a long trip here. So they rest a while; they are checked again and, if necessary, rehydrated. Nam's hot, 110 degrees in the shade, and these kids were carrying sixty and seventy pounds of equipment and ammunition when they got hit. Some of them, too, have been humping it like that for days, if not weeks. They're dehydrated, every one of them. The fluids they get at the 20th give them a bit of an edge. If they're very critical, though, very seriously ill, and can't wait, they're med evac'ed by chopper as soon as they get off the C-141's to one of our four hospitals.

There are nights when everyone is working, and the dispatcher calls about another VSI coming in—type of wound unknown. All of us—the general surgeons, the orthopods, the opthalmologists, and the ear, nose, and throat specialists—go down to the landing pad and wait to see who'll get it. It's a strange sight to see them at two and three in the morning, standing out in the darkened field, some still in their operating clothes, talking quietly, waiting for the sound of the chopper.

If the cases are not critical, the patients go out the next morning on one of the routine chopper runs. The burns go to Kishine; the head and spinal-cord wounds go to the neurosurgical unit at Drake. Ojiie for the most part only takes orthopedic cases. Zama takes them all. The 406th medical laboratory is attached to Zama, and it can do anything from blood gases and fluorescent antibodies to electron micrographs and brain scans. The medical holding company is there too.

The Army likes to pride itself that no one hit in Nam is more than ten minutes away from the nearest hospital. Technically, they're right. Once the chopper picks you up, it's a ten-minute ride to the nearest surg or evac facility, maybe a bit longer if you're really lit up and the med evac has to overfly the nearest small hospital and go on to the closest evac. But the choppers still have to get in and get the troopers out. By the time you read this, over 4000 choppers will have been shot down. More than one trooper will have died in the mud or dust waiting for a med evac that couldn't get in, and there will have been more than one case of a medic having to watch another wounded die on him because he'd run out of plasma and couldn't be resupplied.

If the wounded get to Japan, though, they'll probably live; the survival rate is an astonishing 98 percent. Part of it is the medical care and the facilities in Nam—the incredibly fine care and dedication that go into it. But mostly it's the kind of war we're fighting.

An RPD round travels 3000 feet per second; a 200-pound chicon mine can turn over a 20-ton personnel carrier; a buried 105-mm shell can blow an engine block through the cab of a truck; a claymore sends out between 200 and 400 ball bearings at a speed of 1000 feet per second. For the VC and NVA it's a close-up war. There is nothing very indiscriminate about their killings; it's close-up—booby traps and small arms, ten meters—and they're looking at you all the time.

We had a patient shot through the chest. He was in his hutch when he thought he heard something moving outside. He sat up; the moonlight came in through the door, cutting a path of light across the floor. Sitting up put him in it. The gook was waiting, lying on the ground, no more than two meters from the door. He let off a single round that ripped through the trooper's chest. As he fell back the VC put his weapon on automatic and shot the shit out of the rest of the hutch.

If you're going to die in Nam, you'll die straight out, right where it happens.

If you don't die right out, you've got a pretty good chance; the evac and surgical hospitals do anything and everything. They are linearly set up: triage, X ray, preoperative room, OR, recovery. They are marvelously equipped—twenty seconds from triage to OR—and staffed with competent doctors, who, no matter what they think of the war, do everything they can for its victims. Indeed, there is nothing else to do; it's not France. Even if you have time off, there's no place to go. The 12th evac has six operating rooms and three teams of surgeons. In Nam, if they take you off the choppers alive, or just a little dead, it may hurt a lot, but you'll live.

During Tet, the 12th did seventy major cases a day—everything: wound debridgement, vessel repairs, tendon repairs, abdominal explorations, ventricular shunts, liver resections, nephrectomies, burr holes, chest tubes, amputations, craniotomies, retinal repairs, enucleations. Some-

9

times, even now, they'll have to do four or five major procedures on the same patient. Age helps; the patients are all kids who up until the time they were hit were in the very prime of life. There isn't one who is overweight. None of them, if they smoke, has smoked long enough to eat up his lungs. There are no old coronaries to worry about, no diabetics with bad vessels, no alcoholic livers, no hypertensives. Just get them off the choppers, intubate them, and cut them open. Then they are sent to us here in Japan.

There was a tennis court here once, near the lab building. During the Tet offensive, the fence was torn down and the asphalt used for another helipad. Tet has been over now for some time, but nobody's even thought about putting back the fence. No one mentions it; it is just understood that the court stays a landing pad. It is the way the Army handles its concerns; each individual, of course, handles it his own way. Grieg's developed an ulcer, Dodding is letting his hair grow, Lenhardt sends every patient he can back to Nam; he does it even if he has to extend their profiles 120 days. He's sent troopers back to the paddies with thirteen-inch thoracotomy scars and bits of claymores still in their chests. But he believes in the war and the sacrifice, in the need for making a stand and dying for it if you have to.

Peterson sends everyone he can home, or used to, until he began finding them showing up again in his ward five or six months later. "One laparotomy per country," he'd say. But the Army feels differently, and so there is a pretty good chance that by feeling sorry for these kids and sending them back to the States he's killed a few. A tour in

Nam for an enlisted man is not considered complete unless he has been there ten months, five days. It's considered good time if you are in a medical facility even if you spend your whole tour there—the Army simply counts it as Vietnam time. But if you are in a medical facility, discharged and declared fit for duty, and have served a combined time, either in Nam or in a hospital, of less than ten months, five days, you go back into the computer and if the Army still needs you, you get spit back to Nam. Not for the rest of your tour, but for a complete new twelve months. There are fellows who have been there for a year and a half. It's the Army regulations, and at the beginning Peterson, who thought being an Army doctor was different from being an Army officer, simply didn't spend the time to learn the rules. And so for months he'd profile guys back to the States, where they'd be discharged from the hospitals and returned to Nam.

He tries to hold them now; if they're getting close to the ten-month, five-day deadline, he'll try to extend their profiles thirty days to keep them in the hospital over the deadline. It doesn't go over very big with headquarters, but he's the Doc and you don't need a panel for a thirty-day extension of a temporary profile. You can fool around with the Army if you want and do it very effectively without having to go outside the system; it's all there and ready to use in that formal structure written down in the AR's, which, if definitely applied, would be impossible for anyone to work under. But you have to care, really care, because the Army doesn't like to be fiddled with. You can hold onto patients and refuse to discharge them, clogging up beds in the evac chain. You can put any cold or runny nose you see, no matter what his job, on quarters until every unit commander is screaming. You can demand that the most rigorous rules of hygiene be enforced and drive the senior NCO's crazy. You can ask for a consult on every case, or simply be slow in your dictation until the personnel office is frantic.

The Commander is ultimately responsible for all, and when the patients start piling up at Yokota and the Air Force generals begin to complain, it is he who must answer. At Kishine there was a commander who insisted, despite formal complaints, in interfering with the doctors to the point of demanding that only certain medications be used. He ordered that the "foolishness" be stopped, and everyone obeyed. They discharged their patients, but with a note on the chart that the discharge was under protest, against their medical judgment, and only done under direct orders of the hospital Commander. Everything was put on him, and if indeed anything went wrong anywhere —if a patient died on a plane or even spiked a fever after he'd been discharged, if a cold became pneumonia, if a wound became infected—it would be he who was held responsible. Faced with the possibility of disaster, of being made responsible in fields he really knew nothing about, the Commander backed down and finally left everyone, except his own adjutant, alone.

As a military physician, how you feel about the situation depends on how you look at the war—and, of course, the casualties. Lenhardt, for instance, sees nothing wrong with the war; he says it's better to fight the communists in Vietnam than in Utah. If you see the patients, broken and shattered at eighteen and nineteen as something necessary in the greater scheme of things, then there are no complaints. But if you see these kids as victims, their suffering faces, burned and scarred, their truncated stumps as personal affronts and lifelong handicaps, then you may take a chance on doing what you think is right.

Peterson and Grieg were two of our general surgeons. Hubart and Lenhardt were the other two. They took call every fourth night, and the nights they were on they took all the admissions that day. If they got really bombed, the others just stepped in with them. During Tet and the time the 101st went back into the Ashau, they all came in.

Peterson was on night call in the hospital when the AOD received an emergency call from the Kanto-based air command at Yokota. Because of an accident on the runway, an air evac from Nam scheduled early that morning would have to be diverted to the Naval air station at Atugi, about two miles from Zama. Atugi's runway is shorter than Yokota's, but the pilot had radioed that one of their VSI on board was going sour, and there was some concern whether he would get in country alive. The Air Force and the pilot were willing to take the chance on Atugi, and Atugi agreed. For those flying in Nam, the war doesn't end with the coasts.

The plane landed a little after midnight. It came in under the eerie light of the airstrip with power on, flaps down, its wings almost forty-five degrees to the winds. Touching down on the very edge of the runway, the pilot dumped the flaps, and with the aircraft settling heavily on the concrete, slammed on his brakes, screeching the plane down the runway. Halfway down the strip the brakes began to smolder. With the plane streaming smoke he pulled it into a tight half-turn, and by applying power, skidded it along the edge of the runway until it came to a stop fifty meters from the end of the strip.

The patient was carried to a waiting Navy chopper, which ten minutes later was coming in over the administration building. The usual approach was out over the open fields to the rear of the hospital and then back in again to the landing pad. This pilot took it right in, barely clearing the roof of the building, rattling the windows the whole way in.

Peterson was waiting with the medic near the edge of the pad. The chopper had barely touched down when the crew chief jerked open the door. The inside of the chopper was covered with blood. In the dim half-light of the landing pad it looked like drying enamel.

Peterson and the medic started running onto the pad at the same time. Hunching over to clear the swirling blades, the crew chief helped them into the chopper. The wounded man, his head hanging limply over the edge of the stretcher, was still lashed to the sides of the chopper. Blood welled up from under his half-body cast. Grabbing the top of the plaster cast, Peterson tore it off. A great gush of blood shot up, hit the roof, and then dying, fell away. He put his hand quickly over the wound and pressed down to stop the bleeding; he could feel the flesh slipping away from under his hand. Taking a clamp out of his pocket, he took his hand off the wound and, with the blood swelling up again, stuck the clamp blindly into the jagged hole, worked it up into the groin, and snapped it shut. The bleeding stopped. The chopper, still running, was vibrating around him.

Covered with blood, Peterson yelled to the corpsman to get some O-negative and to call the operating room. Then, with the crew chief, he carried the soldier off the chopper and gave him the first four O-negative units right there on the helipad under the landing lights. By the time they got the patient up to the OR he had some color back.

Peterson operated for two hours. He had to expand the wound, ending up with an incision that ran twelve inches from the front of the patient's thigh, right under his groin, and back around the sides of the leg. When he had cut out the infection and cleaned what he couldn't cut, he had a decent view of the area and carefully went after the artery. Dissecting down through the leg's great vessels and nerves, he found a medium-sized branch of the femoral artery, right above the bone, with a small hole in its anterior surface, and tied it off.

The pathologist from the 406th came in; they had used up all the O-negative blood they had, but it wasn't enough. Half an hour later, a chopper carrying all the O-negative blood at Kishine came in, and two hours later one came in from Drake. It took ten units of blood, but the leg stayed on.

Ten units of blood, though, can do strange things to you. It dilutes normal clotting factors, so that even while you're getting blood, you bleed. Before Peterson had tied off the vessel, the trooper began to ooze from the edges of the wound, then from his nose and mouth. While Peterson worked, Cooper, the head of medicine, opened the blood bank and gave the patient units of fibrinogen and fresh frozen plasma. The bleeding was held in check enough for Peterson to finish up and close the wound. He left the patient to Cooper, and since it was too late in the morning to go to sleep, he went to the snack bar and had some coffee. An hour later he began his morning cases.

Five days later they moved Robert Kurt from the ICU down to the medical ward, where he became Cooper's patient. Peterson had checked him every day while he was in Intensive Care and continued to check on his wound even after he had left the unit. Kurt was quite a bit older than the average soldier, much more alert, and certainly more interesting than the usual adolescent corporal who came through the evacuation chain. He told Peterson he'd been drafted when he had dropped out of his first year of graduate school. It wasn't that he hadn't wanted to go on, he said, it was just that he was getting tired of going to school and wanted to be free for a while. He had taken a chance, and the Army got him.

Two weeks after the operation, Peterson came by and found that someone had put an 101st Airborne patch on Kurt's bed frame.

"You're kidding," he said, staring at the patch.

"No," Kurt said, shrugging. "I figured since I was in it, I might as well really be in it. Besides, I wanted to be with guys who knew what they were doing. I didn't know," he said, smiling good-naturedly, "they would be goddamn crazy."

Peterson nodded, a bit too soberly.

"No," Kurt said, "don't get the wrong idea. They saved

my life. Any other unit, and I'd be dead now. I mean it. I'm glad I was in the 101st."

Peterson didn't look convinced.

"It's the truth. We get hard-core lifers, E-8's and E-9's, captains with direct battlefield commissions, who know fighting. It's their life. When things get hot, they just step in and take over, tell you to get down and wait, this is what's happened and that, and this is what to do. They're calm, and so nobody panics. It's not some storybook thing." He looked down at his leg. "I know I'd be dead now, we'd all be."

Peterson just stood there and let him talk. Apparently Kurt needed to talk, and he let him.

"We got caught—three companies. It must have been an 800-man ambush. They just waited on both sides of us and closed the door on each company—just cut us off from one another. The fire was coming into each company, from all sides, front and back. They really had us. It happens. . . ." He paused, seeing the look on Peterson's face. "And it's going to keep happening. The thing is what happens after you get caught—that's what counts. I was in B Company. If we broke through the gooks in front or in back of us, we'd be running into fire from our own companies, and they were too strong for us to move out to the flanks. We had three artillery batteries of our own working with us, and some of the 1st Air Cav's. No one panicked. We just dug in, found out where we were, and started calling in blocking fire. We were calling it in fifteen meters from our positions. We'd call in a salvo to keep 'em from coming through and one or two rounds farther out to keep 'em from coming around. All the FO's and RTO's

17

from A, B, and C Company were in touch with one another; there wasn't any time to clear the grids. We were
calling in shells on each other, but when an RTO heard
another company calling rounds into the grids they were
in, he had enough sense to pull in his own unit and call
back their location.

"At one time, we were calling rounds ten meters from
each other's positions. That's tough shooting. No one blew.
If we'd panicked . . . I'd be dead. They had us cold for
four hours, but we beat 'em.

"When I got hit, the med evacs couldn't get in. The
colonel just got on the horn and told one of the gunships
to come in and get the wounded. I was bleeding like a
pig. They came in, firing the whole time, picked us up,
took us right in to the TOC CP; they were getting hit too,
but the 101st always carries a surgeon along with them at
the TOC. The gunship must have blasted half the CP
apart to get us in. The Doc clamped my leg and gave me
blood and sent me off again.

"That's the difference, see," Kurt said. "I mean support,
not panic, knowing what you're doing, good officers and
NCO's. The 4th and 25th Divisions would have been
shooting at each other, breaking out into each other's lines
of fire, calling in artillery and gunships all over the place,
and there wouldn't have been a colonel around to give a
shit."

Peterson shook his head.

"I know what you're thinking," Kurt said. "But once
you've hit a village where Charlie's gotten no cooperation,
you sort of get a different view of things. They really kill
'em, the kids and the old people. No, I'm not kidding.

18

We hit three like that. They hang the bodies from the main gate. It makes you think after a while."

"See you tomorrow," Peterson said politely and left. He'd heard it all before, all the reasons. To him it seemed that those in the government had gotten us into a war and then, finding themselves in a bind, not quite sure of themselves, had simply abandoned the problem and left each person to decide for himself. Well, since the options were out, he would use his.

The next morning, he took out half of Kurt's stitches. There was some pus oozing out from the edge of the incision. While Peterson probed the wound, squeezing out the pus pockets, Kurt talked. As Peterson plunged deeper, Kurt gritted his teeth but kept on talking about a trooper who'd frozen on a pull-release bouncing betty.

"But why didn't you help him?" Peterson interrupted as he put down his probe.

Kurt looked up at him, obviously offended. "How?" he said flatly.

"Get him off it," Peterson said, as he put a new dressing on the wound.

Kurt shrugged. "If we could have, we would have. Look," he said seriously, testing his leg, stretching it out a bit more on the bed, "it was a bouncing-betty booby trap. They're all pull-release: you step off it, and then 'boom', the lifting charge goes off and throws the explosive charge up into the air."

"Couldn't you have put something on it and let him step off it?"

"Who you gonna get to do it? The detonator's no bigger than a tit, and you don't know how much pressure you need to hold on it to keep it from going off. Some of them are really unstable. You don't have to step off it to set it off; just shifting your weight can do it. Your foot goes first. You just have to leave them. You have to . . ."

The wound healed nicely, and toward the end of the week Cooper discharged Kurt from the ward and sent him to the medical holding-company barracks, where he could have his physical therapy three times a day without having to stay in the hospital. Peterson gave him the key to his house, and Kurt spent most of his time there, listening to the stereo, reading the magazines, but mostly just taking it easy. After two weeks, his leg was good enough for him to start some slow jogging.

The surgical evacuations were picking up again. Jogging around the hospital area, Kurt was out early one morning when the first med evac choppers began coming in. As they circled slowly around the rim of the fields he watched them, one after another, noting the Red Crosses painted on their noses as they moved in over him.

Peterson never mentioned the evacs to Kurt. They were mostly frag wounds. Some of the kids came in off the choppers with as much as fifty or sixty pieces of steel scattered through their chests and abdomens, and operations lasted five and six hours.

Coming home late one night, Peterson found Kurt sitting quietly on the bench on the front porch.

"Hard day?" Kurt asked, moving over a bit to make room for Peterson to sit down.

"Yeah, they can get sort of long."

In the dim light streaming through the open door they could barely make out each other's features.

"You know," Kurt said quietly, "the only thing that really bothers me about going back—the only thing that really scares me—are those first few weeks." He looked at Peterson. "I've gotten sloppy here; I mean, I'm not sharp anymore. I was running today, some kid came up behind me, and I didn't even hear him. You know," he said, turning back to the dark, "I was out on patrol one night. I heard something, I can't even remember what, or maybe I didn't hear anything, maybe I just felt it. I stopped the patrol and got everyone into a defensive perimeter. We just lay down head to head, and the gooks broke out all around us, must have been a company. They were moving right at us. We were in some deep shit. I don't know why I did it, I did it without thinking. I sent off a round. The echoes screwed 'em up and they moved off again in another direction." Kurt sounded very concerned. "I don't know if I could do it anymore—takes a while to get back into things." He turned to Peterson again. "They would have killed us . . . I'd be dead now. . . ."

The next day, Kurt began pushing himself. In physical therapy they had been using weights on his leg. It was feeling better. He started with short wind sprints and timed miles. His leg kept improving.

Two days after he began sprinting, fifty-eight evacs came in, mostly from the 101st. They had gone back into the Ashau again. Kurt heard about it at lunch, and for the first time since he'd left the ward, he went to the admissions section to see who'd come in. All of them had been badly shot up. Some were already in the OR. A few had been taken right to the Burn Ward; the rest were on the wards.

"You really missed something," one of the men said.

"Yeah?" Kurt said, moving closer to the bed. A corpsman hurried past him.

"Gracie's dead. Got drilled right through the head."

Kurt didn't say anything. What was there to say?

"It was some shit. We couldn't see 'em. They came in behind us, too. Dusty got hit by an RPD, blew him apart. We couldn't even find one of his arms."

"Me?" another friend said, looking down at his own shattered arms. "You're kidding, man. I'm out of it. Worry about yourself."

That night Kurt called Peterson in his office and asked if he could have a sleeping pill. Peterson told him to come by and see him. When Kurt showed up a little past nine, he found Peterson working over his charts.

"Sorry to bother you, doctor," he said apologetically.

"Sit down, sit down," Peterson said, eyeing him keenly. "What's the trouble?"

Kurt remained standing in the middle of the room, tense and withdrawn. "I guess the problem," he said, "the problem is that I know what it's like now. Second times . . ." He fumbled nervously in his pocket for a cigarette. "And getting hit . . . well, you know."

Peterson pointed to the bottle of pills sitting on the edge of his desk.

"Thanks," Kurt said, picking up the bottle.

"Why are you going back?"

Kurt shook out a couple of pills.

"You haven't answered."

22

Kurt shrugged. "I have to."

"No," Peterson said softly, "you don't have to and you know it; you've been around enough to know what can be done and what can't."

Kurt looked at the pills in his hands. "I've got three months left," he said, looking up.

"You've got two weeks. Look," Peterson said, folding his hands on top of his desk. "Everyone's got to decide the important things for themselves. I can't tell you what to do; all I can do is point out a few things."

"I know," Kurt said.

"Do you?" Peterson said. "This war, if anything, is a war of limits and distribution. No one asks that anyone stay in Nam more than a year, no one demands that we bomb beyond a certain line, that we go more than a certain distance—that anyone stay to the end. It's a war of shares, Kurt, and you've done yours. That's all that's asked of anyone or by anyone. I'm not saying whether it's right or wrong, but just how it is. I don't want you killed. You've done enough, you've survived once. I'll extend your profile two more weeks. That will put you over the time limit for a completed tour in Nam, and you can go back to the States. War's over, job's done, tour completed."

Kurt shook his head. "You're making it tough."

"No, Kurt, you are. You've done enough."

"There are a lot of guys still there."

"Yeah, there are. And now it's their turn. You'll be leaving anyway in three months. You going to extend forever until it's over?"

Kurt walked out without answering. Two days later he called the surgical unit and asked for Peterson.

"Telephone, Major," the corpsman said. Peterson left the new evacs and, going over to the desk, picked up the phone.

"Yeah?" he said. For a moment, he had trouble recognizing who it was. "OK, I'll see you in my office in about an hour." He hung up and went back to the evacs. "Well, son," he said, "what happened after the round spun you off the dike?"

Kurt was already in the office when Peterson walked in.

"No, no," Peterson said, motioning for him to keep his seat.

Kurt crushed his half-smoked cigarette in the ashtray beside him and reached into his shirt pocket for another. He looked exhausted, and his hand shook as he lit up. He leaned forward wearily, elbows on knees, holding his head in his hands. "Even with the pills I can't sleep," he said, staring down at the floor. "And I got the shits now, too— and nightmares. The whole damn thing."

Peterson sat down behind his desk.

"It's really gotten to me."

Peterson studied him for a long moment. "Go home, Kurt," he said quietly.

Without looking up, Kurt shook his head.

"I'll call Cooper."

"Don't bother."

"Kurt!" Peterson waited until he lifted his head. "You can always go back if you want. Let it set for a while. See the States, relax, and then if you want, go back. That's all I'm saying."

Kurt took a deep, weary breath.

"OK?"

"Yeah," Kurt said, getting up from the chair. "If you say so."

"I'll tell you what Cooper says."

Peterson picked up the phone and nodded good-bye as Kurt left the room. Cooper was in his office, and the sergeant put the call right through.

"Hi, Dave," Peterson said. "Hear your wards are filling up."

"Hear!" Peterson had to move the phone a bit away from his ear. "They sure are. Someone in Nam decided they're not to have more than 3000 in-patients in country at any one time; might look bad or something like that, so for the next two or three weeks we'll be getting thirty to forty medical evacuations a day. The problem is, where the hell we're going to put them?"

"Want some surgery beds?"

"I'd be happy with a few mattresses," Cooper said. "Anyway, what can I do for you?"

Peterson leaned back in his chair. "Robert Kurt is going back to Nam in a day or two," he said, matter-of-factly. "We were talking, and I found out that he only has five days until his ten months, five days are up. It seems a bit unreasonable to send him back so short."

"He's already been discharged," Cooper said flatly, "and profiled fit for duty."

"I know," Peterson said, "but five days isn't very long. You could extend him just that long for observation."

"That would be a lot of trouble."

"So is three-and-a-half months of getting shot at."

"If you've talked to him," Cooper said curtly, "then you know he's a demolition expert and carries a critical MOS."

"So what?" Peterson hesitated a moment. "What the hell have they been doing over there without him? Stopping the war till he got back?"

"Look," Cooper said into the phone. "That's not the point."

"That is the point," Peterson interrupted.

"Major," Cooper said coldly, "just in case you don't remember, and you obviously don't, the mission of the Army Medical Corps is to support the fighting strength, not deplete it. Right now, there are units running around Nam at three-quarter's strength. That makes every man over there that much less protected and that much more vulnerable. We're at war, whether you or me or anyone likes it or not."

"Then you won't extend him?"

"No!"

Peterson angrily slammed down the phone. Going out into the clinic he told the corpsman to get Kurt.

"When are you supposed to leave?" he asked when Kurt came in.

"I'm manifested for tomorrow morning."

"Listen. I think the best thing to do would be to admit you to my surgical service."

Kurt looked surprised.

"Why? I mean, I thought Colonel Cooper would . . ."

Peterson shook his head. "You've already been discharged from the medical services, and Cooper feels it would look a bit foolish readmitting you or changing your profile even to a temporary one after you've already been cleared, so I'll admit you to my service for an ulcer or something like that."

Kurt looked ill at ease. "You sure there isn't anything wrong?" he asked anxiously.

"No, nothing. We do things like this all the time. Medicine helps us out, and we help medicine out."

"When do you want to see me?"

"I'm admitting you this evening."

Peterson had the ward master tell the hospital registrar to notify the Far East personnel center that Kurt had been admitted and would not be able to make his flight.

The next morning, Cooper called Peterson and told him to come into his office. He stood waiting behind his desk.

"We'll make this short," he said sharply. "Why is Kurt back in the hospital?"

"He may have an ulcer."

"I want that man out of this hospital today."

"He's having gastric distress, relieved by food, and there is a history of possible bloody stools."

"I want him out, I said."

Peterson looked at him calmly, unruffled. "I don't think it would be in the best interests of the Army to send a possible bleeding ulcer back to Nam. It wouldn't look good for this hospital, or any of us, Colonel, to have him sent back here bleeding, especially when he left here with an impression of a possible bleeding ulcer on his chart . . ."

"Has anyone else seen him?" Cooper fumed.

"No, but I don't remember anything in the Army regulations that states a physician has to get an opinion from another physician before admitting a patient to his service, do you? Of course, I could be wrong . . ."

27

Five days later, tests completed, Kurt went home. Peterson took him to Yokota. It was a dark, wet Japanese night. The heavy air hung like a dirty blanket over the plains. They parked their car across from the runway and walked into the terminal, past the unloading gates. There were two med evac C-141's on the runway, unloading their wounded. A thin, cotton-wool mist hung over the edge of the field. In the dim, hazy light, you could barely make out the figures moving across the runway. Overhead, unseen, more C-141's were circling.

One of the patients still out on the runway groaned. Kurt turned anxiously toward Peterson.

"For Christ's sake," Peterson said wearily, "go home, Kurt, will you just go home."

"They're tough. In the Delta we killed
NVA who had walked six months just to
get there, and every day of that trip they
had to take gunships, air strikes, and
B-52 raids. Every day, man, every
fucken day."

Trooper, 9th Division, Riverine Force
Burn Unit
U.S. Army Hospital, Kishine, Japan

2

Mayfield

MAYFIELD lay in the water, listening. He was tired. Not exhausted, just tired out. A single round cracked out from the tree line, but nobody bothered to fire back. Closing his eyes, he tried to relax.

"They're coming, Sarge."

"I know," he said wearily. A few moments later, the gunships swept in over the shore line.

"OK, Otsun. Get 'em ready, we're going home."

They waited, looking over their sights, while the gunships chewed up the tree line. Then, moving out, they began the long walk back to the boats. Mayfield waited until all his men were moving, and giving the smoking tree line one last look, he shouldered his weapon and followed his troopers. Someone else could count the bodies; today he was just too tired, and he wasn't about to lose any more men. The last gunship, cutting playfully low over the paddies, rose suddenly just as it passed over them in some kind of adolescent salute. Shaking his head, Mayfield watched it go.

An hour later they reached the shore and he stopped on a slight rise overlooking the bay. All around, the paddies in crazy checkerboard patterns of green and brown ran right down to the edge of the river. His men, spread out in front of him, were moving slowly through the mud and water, walking cautiously, like hunters moving through a corn field. He didn't know half of them. A first sergeant, and he couldn't keep up with the replacements. Five times in the last week he'd had to bend over the wounded and ask their names. Two had been hit in the head and had lost their tags; nobody even knew who they were, not even the troopers who carried them in. He

31

couldn't keep a second lieutenant; they ran through his fingers like the mud they worked in. He'd lost three that month alone, one right after the other. Finally he'd had to take over the 1st Platoon himself while Clay, the company Commander, took over the 3rd. That way, at least they'd be on opposite sides of a fire fight; if one got hit, the other might be able to hold the unit together. And they were getting hit. Whereas before they'd been running into VC squads, they were running into platoons now and NVA cadre. It was getting tougher all the time.

The tango boats were waiting, motors running, their gun crews nervously looking over their 50's, watching the water line. Thirty meters offshore a hydrofoil, twisted and broken, lay on its side. The troopers, without even bothering to look at it, climbed into the boats. A few, still standing in the water, were already lighting up some grass. Nearby, a Navy helmet was sloshing back and forth in the shallow water. Mayfield, waiting for everyone to get in, stared at it.

"Everybody pays," he thought. "There ain't no place that's safe."

Twenty meters down the shore, Clay, shielding his eyes from the sun, waved at him and climbed into his boat.

At least in Korea he could walk off his hill and relax, Mayfield thought. Disgusted, he threw his M-16 to his RTO and climbed into the platoon's command boat. A few moments later, they were running down the center of the river.

No one talked. They had been out four days, and they hadn't been dry once. They had taken twenty casualties in the same area, whereas just two weeks before they had taken fifteen. Stretching out, Mayfield took a cigarette out of his helmet band and looked at it. Forty-three years old, he thought, and I'm back living on cigarettes and water. His troops lay sprawled around him; two or three were already cleaning their weapons. Mayfield watched them, realizing without the least satisfaction that if they had to they'd go again and again. It wasn't because they wanted to or even believed in what they were doing, but because they were there and someone told them to do it.

Strange war. Going for something they didn't believe in or for that matter didn't care about, just to make it 365 days and be done with it. They'd go, though; even freaked out, they'd go. They'd do whatever he told them. Three mornings in a row after lying in the mud all night, they got up and pushed the gooks back so the choppers could get the wounded out. They charged, every time, just got up and went, right over the RPD's and the AK's. No flags, no noise, no abuse. They just got up and blew themselves to shit because it had to be done. The same with ambushes. They'd do it, and if led right, they'd do it well. But they always let him know somehow that they would rather be left alone; it would be OK if they caught the gooks, but if they didn't, that would be fine too. At first it had been disconcerting—troopers who didn't care but who'd fight anyway, sloppy soldiers smoking grass whenever they could, but would do whatever was asked. Skeptical kids who made no friends outside their own company and sometimes only in their own squads, who'd go out and tear themselves apart to help another unit and then leave when it was over without asking a name or taking a thanks, if any were offered.

It had taken Mayfield a while to get used to, but after a month in Nam he began to realize and then to understand that his troops weren't acting strangely at all, that, if anything, they were amazingly professional. They did what they were supposed to, and it was enough. They had no illusions about why they were here. There was no need for propaganda, for flag waving. Even if there were, these kids wouldn't have bought it. Killing toughens you, and these kids were there to kill, and they knew it. They took their cues from the top, and all that mattered from USARV to the Battalion Commanders was body counts.

He was bewildered the first time he heard a company commander arguing with the S-2 that the four AK's they'd brought in, even though they hadn't found any bodies, meant four kills or at least three. "You can't shoot without a rifle, can you?" he said. "Now, can you?" The killing thing seeped down to every rifleman. Some units were given a quota for the week, and if they didn't fill it, they were just sent out again. He'd heard about units of the 101st burying their kills on the way out and digging them up again to be recounted on the way in. Just killing made it all very simple, and the simplicity made it very professional. Everyone knew the job—even the dumbest kid. The time thing of 365 days just nailed it down; no matter what these kids did or how they acted, they knew they had only 365 days of it and not a second more. To the kids lying around him, Nam simply didn't count for anything in itself. It was something they did between this and that, and they did what they had to to get through it—no more.

Mayfield took off his helmet and let it drop into his lap.

Twenty-six years, and he was out fighting again; he should have been in a division operations, not running a leg company. Somebody had really fucked up. He consoled himself with the thought that only three first sergeants had been killed in Nam.

"Something wrong, Sarge?"

"Nothing," Mayfield said. "Just wondering what it would be like having a desk job in Saigon."

"Dry," someone commented from the front of the boat.

The tango boats moved in a straight line formation down the river. Turning his head, Mayfield looked out through the metal gun slits. The jungle, thick and green, ran right up to the water's edge. After four years of fighting in the Delta it was still all VC. Never again, he thought; not like this, not here. Even if he had to retire. Never again. That much he promised himself.

Their harbor was a number of APB's, APL's, and World War II LST's anchored out in the center of the Miaon River. It was the brigade's base camp. They lived on these boats and deployed from them. If the S-2 found the gooks far from the coast, the choppers took them in. If close, the tangos were used for insertion. It really didn't matter, though; any place in the Delta was wet.

The boat suddenly slowed, and with the engines easing into a heavy rumbling, the men began picking up their gear. A moment later, the boat bumped gently against the hulls of the harbor and, sliding along their sides, came to a stop. Hunched over, the men started moving for the hatches. It was a bright, hot Delta day; the sky, a crystal blue, was almost as difficult to look at as the sun itself. The men climbed out, walked over the metal roofing of

35

the tango boats and up the ladders to the LST's and "apples."

There was no joking; indeed, there was little noise. On deck the company broke up into little groups of no more than four or five. Mayfield walked over to the railing, sat down, and began taking off his boots. While he was untying them, the adjutant came up and told him they'd gotten eleven replacements and he could have them all.

"Any lieutenants?" Mayfield asked, pulling off his soaking boots.

"No, just medics and grunts."

Mayfield began peeling off his socks. "Any ever been here before?"

"No, all cherries."

"OK," Mayfield said, carefully checking his feet. "Get 'em together." He would have liked replacements to get used to the Delta first, but they were short.

The new boys were in little groups toward the bow of the ship. Mayfield introduced himself and asked the married kids to raise their hands, then split them up so they wouldn't be in the same platoon; he didn't want all the married ones killed at once. After dismissing them, he went down to his bunk.

Usually, they were out three days and rested one. That was a grueling enough schedule. Now, with the pick-up in activity, Brigade was cutting that down. It was getting to be three and a half days out and half a day back.

Early the next morning, with only eight hours of rest, they were ordered to move out again. No one complained; as they got ready, a few of the troopers looked suspiciously at their peeling feet, but that was all. Mayfield wrote a quick letter home. He stuffed his usual six packs of cigarettes into his helmet and checked his ammunition clips. They took the things that would matter in a fire fight, nothing else. Nobody bothered with malaria pills; if it hit you malaria was good for six weeks out of the fighting. Nobody darkened his rifle barrel or carried charcoal to blacken his face. The land belonged to the VC. You couldn't kill them unless you found them, which for the most part meant they had to find you.

Only twice in the last four months had they surprised the gooks. The first time was on a sweep near Quang Tri; they were crossing some high ground. It was early in the morning, and they caught them sitting behind a hedgegrove, eating. They even had their weapons stacked. The Captain had waited until the whole company was on line, and then they had killed them all. Forty-seven, just like that.

The second time was a month later. Mayfield's platoon had tracked a VC squad for three days, keeping after them until they caught them in the middle of a paddy. Such things were good for morale, but they didn't happen often.

This morning they were inserted by chopper. The slicks moved them inland, keeping above 1500 feet. Two kilometers from the LZ, they dipped down and came in right over the paddies. The pilot and the door gunners cleared their weapons, and two of the accompanying cobras moved out ahead and a little to the side. It was 100 degrees when they hit the LZ.

With the slicks in line, hovering a few inches above the paddy water, the troops jumped off, moving away in a crouch to keep the prop wash from blowing them over.

During the insertion, the gunships and cobras circled in protective lazy spirals in and out over the landing zone. Finally the slicks pulled out, and the gunships gave the area one last look, then pulled out after them and followed them back to the boats. Regrouped and moving out, the men, already soaked with sweat, began walking through the filthy water, some for the hundredth time. After the roaring of the choppers, the tinkling of the men's gear sounded almost musical. A radio squawked and just as quickly was cut off.

"Otsun," Mayfield said matter-of-factly. The RTO turned around. "Tell the men, that if I hear one more radio, I'll shoot the son of a bitch myself. Understand?"

The platoons separated so that there were at least 200 meters between each of them, in staggered columns: tiger scouts up ahead, points, and then the main body of almost a hundred men pushing through the muggy heat of the Delta. By noon they were passing little villages, no more than a few wooden huts, built behind mud dikes. Some of the villagers came out to watch them go by. Everyone looked alike, friends and enemies. The little old woman standing next to her hut could have just that morning changed the batteries on the land mines, which might that evening be blowing them to shit. It was hard to like them anyway; it was hard to like anything in that heat.

The whole time Mayfield had been in the Delta he hadn't gotten one piece of information out of these people. The only consolation was that they might be just as close-mouthed with the VC. Maybe, from what he'd been told, the VC they'd been helping, or at least not hindering, had really pushed them around at Tet and were still pushing them, killing chiefs and stealing kids. You couldn't be sure; the truth probably lay somewhere between, like the mud bunkers the villagers had built near their huts. They were there for protection against gunships as well as Charlie—whoever was around at the time. The only thing Mayfield was sure of in all that suffocating heat was that the Army wasn't winning these people for anything.

They had walked for almost five hours; the sun on an angle reflected blindingly off the shallow paddy water. Mayfield, halting on the edge of a hedgegrove—his troopers already moving out into the next paddy—stopped for a moment to put on his sunglasses.

The first mortar round hit fifty meters to his right. Even as he was diving off the hedgegrove, automatic fire was cracking into the mud around him. Mortars were going off all around; a string of bullets hit near the side of his face, slapping mud up into his eyes. Twisting, he began crawling as fast as he could away from the slapping sound of the bullets. He was crawling blindly, arms and legs digging frantically into the soft mud, when he felt a sharp blow against his upper arm, like a baseball bat hitting him across the shoulder. Changing direction, he quickly began rolling over and over, perpendicular to the way he'd been crawling. There was noise and confusion all around. Covered with mud, choking on it, he kept rolling to his left. A mortar round or rocket hit somewhere above his head, the concussion driving his helmet down onto the bridge of his nose. Stunned, he stopped his frantic rolling. When the pain cleared, he could hear the rattling of RPD's somewhere up ahead, the firing of AK's everywhere. They'd been caught out in the open. Rolling onto his stomach, he wiped the mud out of his eyes; NVA, he thought, pulling up his M-16 so he could fire it.

"Otsun!" he yelled.

An RPG sputtered across the paddy, exploding on a rise off the left.

"Over there, dammit, over there! There, goddammit!" he yelled, emptying his own weapon into the hedgegrove directly in front of them. It was about fifteen meters away. The fire from the boys in the paddy shifted into the grove. Suddenly the middle of the grove exploded, sending out streaks of burning frags and bushes in all directions. "Take it!" Mayfield yelled, and springing up, still screaming, he was charging toward the grove when a round hit his pack and spun him off his feet. But the platoon was moving, concentrating their fire even while he was struggling to get back to his feet. They were moving past him; they took the grove with less than twenty boys standing. They had some cover now, but the other sides of the contact were still pouring fire into the paddies.

Mayfield yelled for Otsun again. A corporal, covered with mud, a bandolier of filthy M-60 ammunition slung across his chest, pointed toward the front of the grove. Otsun was face down in the mud, the radio still strapped to his back. A mortar round hit behind the grove. A soldier broke for the radio. Slipping down the side of the grove he reached the RTO and was pulling off the radio when a round caught him in the head and pitched him backward. Another trooper rolled out of the tangle, reached Otsun, grabbed the radio, and yanking it free threw it into the grove. Mayfield crawled after it, checked it, and put it on its base. Hunched over, with rounds cracking through the grove, he switched the radio on to the command net. Nothing. He checked it quickly again to make sure it was working and twirled the dials. Suddenly he realized that all the RTO's could have been killed outright or their radios destroyed. It could have happened; a waving antenna is an inviting target. They might have been the first to go. It was a good enough ambush for that.

Mayfield pressed the button. A tracer rough spun off the top of the grove. Someone behind him was screaming for a medic. Looking out through the bushes he checked the paddy. That early mortar round had saved them.

"River 6/River 18," he said into the microphone. "River 18/River 6. 6/18, we're taking heavy automatic fire; RPG's and mortars; probably NVA. Grid 185/334 heavy automatic fire. 18/6 leaving freq to air support freq, leaving your push now." Mayfield looked around; the gooks were in the groves in front of them, behind them, and to their flanks. "You!" he yelled, waving over one of the troopers. He sent the grenadiers to their flanks with orders to use shotgun rounds, and was giving orders for the placements of the M-60's when the radio crackled.

"18/6, four phantoms up at 40 right near you, switch to air-support freq code named Thunderchief."

Mayfield switched the dials. There was no SOP for the 4's; you just talked to them.

He pressed the horn button. "Thunderchief, 18."

"18, this is Thunderchief. Be over you in two minutes."

A VC moved out of the grove on their right. Mayfield was reaching for his weapon when one of his troopers stood up and emptied his M-16. The bushes around the gook were torn apart and, spinning around with the torn leaves, he tumbled into the mud. Mayfield pulled his gun closer to him, but left it on the ground.

"18, this is Thunderchief," the radio said. "Air currents too heavy. Diving . . . Now!"

Still holding the horn, Mayfield picked a smoke canister out of his webbs, pulled the pin, and threw it out in front of the grove. He took out another smoke grenade and threw it to the left. The thick smoke curled back over them.

"18," the radio crackled, "where the fuck are you? OK, see you, green smoke."

Mayfield picked up the microphone, "Roger, green, request first round W.P."

"Roger, 18. Coming in from the west. Get your heads down."

Mayfield dropped the horn. "Tac Air!" he yelled, "Tac Air!" The cry was carried up and down the grove. Taking off his helmet, he pushed himself flat on the ground and, burying his face in the dirt, covered his ears. Everyone was doing the same thing.

"18," the radio squawked, "see the smoke." A second later a phantom came roaring in over the grove, no more than fifty feet off the ground. The sound was deafening; even with his hands over his ears, the noise was painful. The earth vibrated, and then the air seemed to be sucked up from the ground. A moment later, the ground heaved up into his face, and with a dull shock the explosions, carrying dirt and rocks, passed over them. Without lifting his head, Mayfield picked up the horn.

"Thunder/18, Shell H and E; repeat, Shell H and E."

"18/Thunderchief," the voice answered. "Roger that."

The second phantom came in even lower. Pressed into the ground, Mayfield saw the shadow pass by, heard the same deafening roar, and this time the incredible explosions of H and E.

"Once more," the voice said lightly. "I still see something moving. Hang on, coming around again."

A dirty haze from the explosions rose up in front of the grove, blocking out the sun. All the firing had stopped. They came in together this time—six yards apart, four feet off the ground. Mayfield dug in even deeper. The tangle of the hedgegrove was blown apart by the jet's exhausts. Then, roaring over, shattering the air, the planes passed. A moment later the heat and concussions of the explosions seared past them, burning the tops of the grove. Mayfield looked up and, through the dirt, saw the two planes already a half mile away, still on the deck, beginning to bank to the right and left.

The hedgegroves in front and to the sides were flaming wrecks. To his left, he could hear the whooshing of incoming artillery. Mayfield switched to the command net. It was bursting now: Red Legs, Dust Offs, Tac Air—they were giving casualties out in the open. Mayfield couldn't recognize one voice; the Old Man in the C and C chopper was overhead, taking care of the whole thing. Behind them the firing was picking up again.

The medics had carried the wounded into a clear space toward the back of the grove. Mayfield, watching them stack the dead, was just getting up when a rocket hit right in the middle of the area, and the concussion knocked him over again. Numbed, he struggled back to his feet. Around the aid station the bodies were sprawled all over the place. He could hear the gunships whooping in off to his left. Still dazed, he pressed the button. He had been holding onto the horn the whole time.

"Priority one, this is River 18." He repeated it without waiting for an acknowledgment. "Need Dust Off, urgent."

The Old Man cut in, "River 18/6, switch to air-evac net."

Mayfield had trouble moving his arm. "Dust Off, this is River 18, urgent." While he was talking he stared at the shambles that had been the aid station. Some of the men had already left the perimeter to help; there were cries all around for medics. They must have all been hit, he thought. The VC were dropping rounds everywhere. He was counting slowly to himself, totaling up the casualties, trying to be accurate. He pressed the button: "Fifteen wounded; repeat, fifteen wounded—eight, ten, critical."

The radio crackled, "River 18, this is Dust Off 4. Is the area secure?"

"Negative." An M-60 opened up again on his flank.

"Roger, River 18, coming in. River 18, can you give me smoke?"

"Negative," Mayfield said. "I have you visual, will direct you in." He couldn't afford to give the gooks a better target than they already had. The mortar might have been luck; but it also might not have been. He stayed on the horn, directing them in. The first Dust Off came in, gliding in over the paddies. Just as he saw it breaking, he heard the 51 open up. The pilot ignored the bullets and took his chopper right through the stream of tracers. At the last moment, just as he was settling it in, the machine wavered and then, stricken, twisted over on its side and, rotating slowly about its center, cartwheeled gracefully out over the paddy. The tip of its main rotor hit the mud. A second later it exploded, burning up in a bright flash of igniting magnesium. Two gunships on the perimeter moved in and hit the area of the 51 with machine-gun fire, racking it apart. Another Dust Off bore in, this time at a steeper angle. Mayfield worked the horn, keeping the gunships close so that the Dust Off could get in. He could see more slicks crossing the horizon. The fighting seemed to be moving off to the east.

The second med evac made it in, and they loaded on the bodies. A loach circled protectively overhead, and, higher up, a cobra circled in the opposite direction. While they were loading, Mayfield plotted out artillery targets—just in case—and sent in the coordinates. He didn't have enough men standing to stop anything. If anything happened, he would have to plaster the area with artillery, and he wouldn't have time to call in the coordinates while he was doing it. He ordered the batteries to stand ready to fire on his command. Meanwhile, the company was sorting itself out. The air strikes had settled things down, and now only an occasional sniper round came through.

"Hey, Sarge."

"Yeah."

"Better take care of that arm."

Mayfield looked down at his shoulder. His fatigues were ripped, and his skin was caked black with dirt and blood.

Testing his arm, he found he could still move it a bit. He waited by the horn until he was sure they'd be OK— they'd pull out. Getting up, he walked through the mud to what had been the aid station. The dead, partially covered with muddy ponchos, were again stacked in piles. The wounded, filthy and dirty, were laid out next to them, with blank, empty looks on their faces.

A trooper kneeling next to one of the wounded was trying to start an IV. The medic, the only corpsman alive, flack vest open, moved from patient to patient. Two soldiers, their weapons cradled exhaustedly in their arms, were just sitting near the wounded. Mayfield, dragging himself, plodded up through the mud that was strewn with broken bits of albumin cans.

"Sarge!"

A trooper, walking up to him, slipped and barely kept his balance, splattering mud all over him. "Sorry," he said apologetically. "The RTO from 3rd Platoon says the choppers are coming."

"I know," Mayfield said. He looked around him. As dirty as it was and as hot, he didn't want to go. Sweating and exhausted, he didn't want to leave—not right away, anyway. They'd fought for this mud, his men had died for it; he wanted something to show for it all. He didn't want to have to keep bringing them back to it again and again. He wanted to stay; they'd won it.

"Sarge."

"Yeah."

"The Old Man says to get ready; as soon as the wounded and dead are out, we're moving back to the boats."

46

———

"When I get there I'm gonna ask to fly
med evacs. I mean, I know they need
pilots to fly guns, but I'd just rather not."

Chopper pilot
En route Vietnam
Travis Air Force Base, California

———

3

Medics

A T Zama we read in the stateside papers that America was going to hell, that it was almost impossible to get an American teenager to act responsibly, listen to an adult, or, for that matter, even to care. You'd think, then, that it would be impossible to get them to kill themselves for something as vague as duty or run through claymores for anything as subtle as concern. But during the first five hours of Hamburger Hill, fifteen medics were hit, ten were killed. There was not one corpsman left standing. The 101st had to CA in medics from two other companies, and by nine that night, every one of them, too, had been killed or wounded.

Graham was eighteen years old when a tracer round skidded off his flack vest and triggered a grenade in his webbing. He struggled for a moment to pull it off and then, according to the other medic working with him, he jumped out of the aid station, and kept running, with the grenade bouncing against his chest until it went off.

Pierson, nineteen, was at the rear of his squad when the buried 105 blew. He hit the ground with everyone else, but when the explosion wasn't followed up with small arms fire, he got up and began running toward the settling dust. The smell of cordite still stung the air. Three troopers had been blown off the track. One had the whole bottom half of his body sheared off; the second lay crumpled against a tree, a huge gaping hole in the very center of his chest; the third, half of his bottom jaw blown off, lay flapping around on the ground, blood gushing out of his neck and spilling into what was left of his mouth.

Pierson wrestled him quiet. While the rest of the squad hurried by, he took out his knife and, grabbing the protruding piece of jaw bone, forced back the soldier's head and calmly cut open his throat, then punched a hole into the windpipe. A sputtering of blood and foam came out through the incision, and as his breathing eased, the soldier quieted.

There was another explosion up ahead and the rattling of small arms fire. Taking an endotracheal tube out of his kit, Pierson slipped it in through the incision and threaded it down into the soldier's lungs, listened for the normal inward and outward hiss of air, then reached for the morphine. One of the troopers who had come up from a trailing squad was checking the other bodies. "Hey, Doc," he said, "these two are dead." Without looking up, Pierson shoved the needle deep into the soldier's arm and drove the plunger smoothly down the barrel of the syringe.

Webb had been in Nam only three days when he got into his first fire fight. The 3rd Platoon working out ahead had killed three dinks near a bridge. A few hundred meters farther they found a small arms cache with four AK-50's, a couple of RPD's, and a Smirnov attack rifle. They waited for the rest of the company and then they all moved out through the waist-high grass. You could feel trouble coming; up and down the line the troopers switched their weapons to automatic and shifted their rucksacks so they could drop them more easily. The machine gunners began carrying their weapons at port arms instead of across their shoulders. The grenaders loaded their M-79's with cannister rounds. Up ahead, fifty meters away, was a thick tree line. The only sound was the company moving through the grass and an occasional tinkle of loose gear. Webb was walking with the Sergeant.

"Thirty meters," the Sergeant said softly. "We'll get hit inside of thirty meters."

"Sooner," a trooper offered drily. Twenty meters farther the firing began. Even as he hit the ground, Webb saw three figures tumble over in front of him. Within seconds the whole field was exploding. Automatic fire cracked and snapped through the dry grass. An RPD hidden off to the right began firing and caught a squad trying to move off that way. Two other machine guns opened up on the left. Seeing where they were falling, the gooks began skipping rounds into them.

Behind and overhead, Webb could hear the gunships thumping their way toward them. The VC stopped firing as the first loach, small and agile, swept in over their heads. A moment later a cobra swung in. Everybody was popping smoke grenades. Webb got to his knees and, seeing a trooper dragging a body toward a nearby rise, shook off his rucksack. Taking his helmet off and leaving it on the ground with his M-16, he got to his feet and began running toward them with his aid kit. He made ten meters before they got him: a clean straight round that caught him under his swinging left arm and came out the other side of his chest.

In the Ashau, an RPG landed next to the CP and buried itself in the ground before it exploded. Ignoring the explosion, the medic was reaching up over the trooper to open the albumin can he had just hung when an RPD swept the area. The first burst shredded through his flack vest, lifting him up and spinning him around before it dropped him back to earth five feet away.

Watson had been a troublemaker since he was six. He was a bitter, imaginative, hate-filled kid who had been drafted and somehow had survived basic training without ending up in prison. He was assigned to the medics at an evac hospital and then to the field. When he went on line, the hospital personnel gave him a week to be busted and sent back to the States in irons.

When I met him he had been up front with his unit for almost five months. He was soft-spoken, but marvelously animated and alert. The old abusiveness was gone; even the adolescent arrogance I'd been told had for so long been the central pillar of his personality had disappeared. He was perfectly at ease and open. Those who had known him before were pleasantly surprised, if still a bit leery.

Watson didn't mind talking. "Why not go all out, man? They need me, and I know what I'm doing out there. Hundreds of cases—fucken hundreds. The big-shot dermatologists, they come down once a week. They look at all that rotting skin and shake their heads and leave. Know what we done? We got a mix-master, threw in a couple of quarts of calamine lotion, a few kilograms of mycolgue for the fungus, and figured some tetracycline and penicillin couldn't hurt, just in case there was any bacteria around. Called it jungle mix and bottled it and handed it out. Fucken dermatologists couldn't believe it. Wanted to know where we'd read about it, what medical journal. Sure, I take chances. That's my job—to save lives. The VC—well, I ain't got nothing against 'em. Guess they're doing their job, too."

On a routine sweep through Tam Key, a squad of the Americal Division was ambushed. Watson was hit twice, both rounds shattering his leg. He kept helping the wounded, dragging himself from soldier to soldier until he was hit in the neck by a third round and paralyzed.

All the medics talk the same and they all act the same, whether they come from the ghetto or from the suburbs. No one planned it this way. It was the kids themselves, caught between their skeptical seventeen or eighteen years, and the war, the politicians, and the regular Army officers. Growing up in a hypocritical adult world and placed in the middle of a war that even the dullest of them find difficult to believe in, much less die for, very young and vulnerable, they are suddenly tapped not for their selfishness or greed but for their grace and wisdom, not for their brutality but for their love and concern.

The Army psychiatrists describe it as a matter of roles. The adolescent who becomes a medic begins after a very short time to think of himself as a doctor, not any doctor in particular, but the generalized family doctor, the idealized physician he's always heard about.

The excellent training the medics receive makes the

whole thing possible, and the fact that the units return the corpsman's concern and competence with their own wholehearted respect and affection makes the whole thing happen.

Medics in the 101st carried M & M candies in their medical kits long before the psychiatrists found it necessary to explain away their actions. They offered them as placebos for their wounded who were too broken for morphine, slipping the sweets between their lips as they whispered to them over the noise of the fighting that it was for the pain. In a world of suffering and death, Vietnam is like a Walt Disney true-life adventure, where the young are suddenly left alone to take care of the young.

A tour of Nam is twelve months; it is like a law of nature. The medics, though, stay on line only seven months. It is not due to the good will of the Army, but to their discovery that seven months is about all these kids can take. After that they start getting freaky, cutting down on their own water and food so they can carry more medical supplies; stealing plasma bottles and walking around on patrol with five or six pounds of glass in their rucksacks; writing parents and friends for medical catalogues so they can buy their own endotracheal tubes; or quite simply refusing to leave their units when their time in Nam is over.

And so it goes, and the gooks know it. They will drop the point, trying not to kill him but to wound him, to get him screaming so they can get the medic too. He'll come. They know he will.

"We get a distorted picture over here in Japan. We see the guys after they've been fixed up a bit and acclimated to their injuries. Over there it's a kid suddenly full of holes. You're faced with the stark reality of it—not just a sick patient, but a dying healthy kid who's just been blown apart."

Chief of Surgery
Staff meeting
U.S. Army Hospital, Camp Zama, Japan

4

Final Pathological Diagnosis

THE Chicom mines the VC and NVA use are plastic. They hold ten pounds of explosive charge and three pounds of fragments. They can be pressure-detonated, and the explosive charge can be set for whatever pressure is wanted—a tank, a jeep, a truck, or a person. If the mines are placed right they can blow an engine block through the hood or turn over an APC. Since the bombing halt, though, there have been enough to waste a few on recon patrols.

This one must have been a pull-release. It blew after he stepped off it—throwing him ten feet into the air. When the medic finally reached him, his left leg was already gone, and his right leg was shredded up to his thigh. The blast had seared through the bottoms of his fatigues, burning his penis and scrotum as well as the lower part of his abdomen and anus. The medic gave him morphine and started albumin. A Dust Off was called in, which took him to the twenty-seventh surgical hospital near Quang Tri, where they took off his testicles and penis, explored his abdomen, took out his left kidney and four inches of large bowel, sewed up his liver, and did a colostomy and right ureterostomy. During the procedure he was given twenty units of uncrossed O-positive blood.

After three days at the twenty-seventh, he was evacuated to Japan via the Yokota Air Force base. From Yokota he was taken by chopper to the U.S. Army hospital at Camp Zama. His left leg was removed by a left-hip disarticulation, and his right thumb and left index finger were sutured. There was not enough skin to close his surgical wounds completely, so his stumps were left open. Despite antibiotics, his wounds became infected. The fourth night in the ward he tried to kill himself. On the sixth day his urinary output began to diminish, and the laboratory began culturing bacteria out of his blood stream. On the seventh day his fever hit 106 degrees Fahrenheit; he became unconscious, and seven days following his injuries he expired. His body was then transferred to the morgue at Yokota airbase for shipment back to the continental United States.

FINAL PATHOLOGICAL DIAGNOSIS

1. Death, eight days after stepping on a land mine.
2. Multiple blast injuries.
   A. Traumatic amputation of lower extremeties, distal right thumb, distal left index finger.
   B. Blast injury of anus and scrotum.
   C. Avulsion of testicles.
   D. Fragment wounds of abdomen.
   E. Laceration of kidney and liver, transection of left ureter.
3. Focal interstitial myocarditis and right heart failure.
   A. Left and right ventricular dilation.
   B. Marked pulmonary edema, bilateral.
   C. Marked pulmonary effusion, bilateral (3000 cc in the left, 1500 in the right).
   D. Congestion of lungs and liver.
4. Patchy acute pneumonitis (Klebsiella-Aerobactoer organism).
5. Gram negative septicemia.
6. Extensive acute renal tubular necrosis, bilateral.
7. Status post multiple recent surgical procedures.

Final Pathological Diagnosis

A. Hip disarticulation with debridgement of stumps, bilateral.
B. Testicular removal bilaterally.
C. Exploration of abdomen, suturing of lacerated liver.
D. Removal of left kidney and ureter.
E. Multiple blood transfusions.

EXTERNAL EXAMINATION

The body is that of a well-developed, well-nourished, though thin, Negro male in his late teens or early twenties, showing absence of both lower extremities and extensive blast injuries on the perineum. There is a large eight-inch surgical incision running from the chest wall to the pubis. There is a previous amputation of the distal right thumb and left index finger. . . .

"I liked it better in '65 and '66. Then it was just you against them. Now you just sit back and you get blasted away or they do. That ain't no fun."

Special Forces trooper
Orthopedic Ward
U.S. Army Hospital, Kishine, Japan

5

The Shaping-Up of McCabe

MCCABE wrote his story about Vietnam during the fall term of his senior year, two months after he'd returned from ROTC summer camp. It was not a very good story, but he liked it, and the school's literary quarterly published it. They had published a few of his other things—lyrical little pieces about growing up—which had earned him a certain literary notoriety. It had caused a bit of a flap among the campus intellectuals when he enrolled in ROTC, but there was a war on, and he wanted to have a piece of it. Hemingway had his Spain; McCabe would have his Vietnam.

But Nam was not at all like his story, nor really what he had hoped for. In the twenty-seven days he had been there, the only village he had ever come near was the one he blew away. Women, children, dogs, huts, rice, water buffalo—the whole thing. He just sat there on his track half a click away and blew it apart. He did it two weeks after he'd been in country, and the fourth night after his unit had been hit three nights in a row.

The morning before McCabe destroyed the village, a squad sweeping through the village area found the imprints of mortar tubes 500 meters from the village. The Old Man asked for clearance to hit the compound but was told that unless they were receiving direct fire, they were to leave it alone. That evening he told McCabe that on the first round that came in from anywhere—anywhere—he was to blow the village off the face of the map.

Before it got dark, McCabe plotted the village's coordinates and pasted them on the front of his radio. A little after midnight, they took a single sniper round. The bullet cracked across the lager and was gone. While troopers turned over in the mud and tried to get back to sleep, McCabe, shaking himself awake, climbed up on his track. In the silence, he picked up the horn and, staring out into the black, cloudless night, called in an illumination round. Fifteen seconds later it came whistling in over his head, splattering the paddies into a dazzling, metallic silver. The star shell drifted gently in the air and swung slowly back and forth above the village. With the radio crackling in the heavy air, McCabe waited a while to make sure the star shell was working, then pressed the button.

"69/51 fire mission, over."

"69 fire mission, out."

He checked the coordinates and then looked back at the village.

"51 D.T. 106 direction 0600; shell H and E, enemy visible; prox 800 meters, over."

"51/69 corrective, shell WP, over."

"69/51," he said calmly; "shoot, over."

"51 shoot, out,"

The first rounds came roaring in over the lager. Suddenly, with a reddish roar, the whole left side of the compound lifted up.

"69/51, right 50, add 100; shell H and E; request zone fire, three quadrant, 3 mills, battery 2, over."

The radio crackled again with the corrective read back, and a minute later a second salvo came roaring in. The center of the village was suddenly gone. Hundreds of square meters of ground were being thrown into the air, tumbling over, twisting, in a conflagration of noise and fire. Far away he could see tiny figures running out of what was left of the village.

The Shaping-Up of McCabe

"69/51 mixed shell H and E and WP. Air burst—20 meters."

White hot steel and phosphorous slammed down into the ground, taking everything and everyone with it.

When it was over, McCabe's RTO patted him on the back. He put away his grids. This was not his kind of war; he would rather have been on his own, close up without all this noise and confusion. With the illumination round fading in front of him into a soft yellow green, he picked up his M-16 from the top of the track, climbed down from his APC, and began walking around the lager, checking the perimeter defenses.

He walked slowly past the great hulking thirty- and forty-ton shapes. Walking up alongside a tank he stopped, put his hand on it, and looked out at the razor wire. The steel, grimy from the mud, was still warm from the day's sun. Drawing his hand thoughtfully along the armor, he walked on past the tracks and stood quietly near the driver's hatch, the cannon reaching out silently above his head. Slinging his weapon, he took his hand off the armor and wiped it clean, He was still surprised—even after two weeks—at having been assigned as a forward observer to a mechanized unit. Even with a primary MOS of an artillery officer, he hadn't expected it. He had gone into the artillery during ROTC because he wanted to be part of a combat arm, and artillery was the only one the school offered. He thought he'd left artillery behind him at Fort Sill. He had complained, but no one at the 90th Replacement would listen. "We don't need Rangers," they said. "We need forward observers."

It was not an uncommon occurrence in Nam; Rangers

are dispersed through the Army. There are no Ranger units as such. The Army doesn't like elite troops; they've always felt them to be more trouble than they were worth. The training, though, is good, so the Pentagon offers it, but then disperses the men in different units, officially to act as leavening for the rest of the Army, though unofficially to keep these highly trained elite men from getting together and feeling special.

McCabe was disappointed. He would have liked to have used what he had learned. It was not just a romantic notion; Florida had killed the last of his fantasies. What advanced infantry training, Fort Sill, jump school, and Fort Benning hadn't done, the swamps had.

The day after graduation from college, McCabe was out of ROTC and on active duty, on his way to Fort Sill, Oklahoma, where the Army was sending him to learn more about artillery. He felt he was going as an interested observer rather than as a second lieutenant. At first he kept a little notebook, but after a while he gave it up, consoling himself that what he couldn't remember later wouldn't be worth writing down now.

At Fort Sill his first impression—one that never quite left him—was how big it was: not only Fort Sill but the Army itself. Sill was a country within a country. But it was more than the sheer physical size that affected him; it was the way the Army sat there, reaching out across the whole country, grabbing everyone and pulling people into it without the slightest concern for what they were, what they wanted to be, or what they did. Those first few days, watching it function, unique and insular, saluting and being saluted, he marveled at how something that big and complex, something affecting so many people's lives, could have been there all along, without his even knowing it. It was difficult to get used to, and if the cadre hadn't been so serious about it all, the regimentation and the foolishly exacting concerns would have been laughable. But it was business, serious business, and they got right to it, quickly, with little humor.

"OK," the instructor said, "you are officers. It is our job here at Fort Sill to make you artillery officers, so we shall start at the beginning."

Survey, phone communication, laying the base piece, laying the battery, setting up the FDC, setting up the exec post, registering the guns, grids, firing from fixed points, scales, tables, logarithms, trigonometry—it went on every day: lectures, texts, discussions, reviews.

"Gentlemen," the Major said, standing in front of the demonstration table until the class was completely quiet, "there are four kinds of fuses. Point detonating: it will," he said, pointing to the first cone-shaped tube in front of him, "detonate on contact, though the pressure necessary for that detonation can be varied. Timed"—he pointed to the second—"the times can be changed—two seconds out of the barrel, five seconds. Delayed"—he picked up the third—"if the leg units are pushing the enemy, and they're turning but don't have a blocking force on the flanks, you can lay shells with these fuses into the flanking areas. These time fuses can be used as an instant mine field, any delay you want. This one," he said, pointing toward the fourth, "this is the beauty—variable time. It is radar-controlled. On its way down, impulses are sent out from the detonator, and the time it takes these impulses to get back to the falling shell is measured and computed, and when the time span is equal to whatever height you've set, it will detonate."

He waited a moment. "You just set the range on the fuse for whatever height you want. Set the fuse for the height of twenty meters, and it will flatten everything within fifty meters."

"Gentlemen," the Major said the next day, the Oklahoma landscape shimmering behind him as he stood by the small platform at the base of a howitzer, "there are four kinds of shells: high explosive, white phosphorous, smoke, and anti-personnel. This," he said, pointing to a shell standing on the platform in front of him, "is an anti-personnel round. It was developed after Korea, and it will stop your batteries from being overrun. Inside each shell are 10,000 feathered stainless-steel darts. It is detonated by a specially timed fuse that sets itself when the shell is spinning at 1500 rpm's. This is approximately the rpm's the fired shell will be rotating at when it has traversed half the barrel length of a 105-mm howitzer. In the time it takes to traverse the rest of the barrel length, the fuse detonates, and the shell casing, of special construction, twirls off the round much as the casing off a can of sardines. By the time the round leaves the barrel, the casing is completely gone, and the 10,000 darts come blowing out the barrel." He stopped for a moment. "Just crank down the gun to zero elevation . . ."

McCabe stared at the cannon, anchored so firmly into the ground in front of him.

"Now, gentlemen," the Major said, "we are scheduled this hour to talk about FADAK—the artillery computer. It can, as you know, read maps, terrain, weather conditions, meteorological situations. It can register your gun, and if you want, it can shoot it."

During the whole time not one instructor specifically mentioned Nam; they stayed away from any mention of killing and death, though there were allusions, such as, "Most of you will be using grid coordinates for your fire missions; locations from known points are used only in the European theater of operations" and "White phosphorous should be considered as much a psychological weapon as a pyrogenic one."

The classroom work went on for two weeks, with officer training in between. McCabe was getting bored and a bit fed up with the academics of it all. It was getting to be just like college all over again. But things changed when they went out to the artillery range, a great hilly area at the eastern edge of the fort. They went in their combat gear. After a four-mile hike and a quick talk on safety procedures, they took up their positions. McCabe was given the first fire mission. With the class spread out behind him, he lay down on the rim of a high hill overlooking the huge, desolate, pock-marked Oklahoma valley baking in the sun. He opened his grids and, laying them down on the dirt next to him, took the horn from the RTO. He was given a convoy in the open.

"59/51 fire mission, over." He waited, and pressing the button, went on. "Grid 524/313, direction 0300, shell WP, convoy in the open, over."

"51 fire mission, out."

"Fire mission—524/313; 0300—out."

And two miles behind him a battery of 105-mm how-itzers began traversing toward the target.

"59/51 grid 524/313 clear."

Less than a minute later, a single shell came whistling in over his head. Despite himself, he was startled by how quickly it was over him and how loud it sounded—like a freight train roaring down through a narrow canyon. A moment later it exploded. A white puff rose out in the val-ley. Almost right on, he thought; a bit too high, though. Excited, lying sweating on his hill, he pressed the button again, with the guns working unseen miles behind him, doing whatever he asked. He felt somehow as if he were conjuring up the Devil.

"59/51 L50 drop 200, shell H and E. Request battery fire for effect. At my command." He waited a moment, looked out expertly at the valley, and then, putting down his binoculars, gave his grids one more look and ordered: "Fire!"

Almost instantly a salvo came roaring over. Unconsciously he ducked his head. He had his glasses fixed on the smoke from the first round. Suddenly the ground, a good 500 meters behind the white marking smoke of the first round, heaved open, and the dull thud-ding of the exploding shells rolled back over him. Confused, McCabe looked quickly from his grids to the smoking valley and back again.

"You killed at least a company of our own men," the Sergeant said, kneeling down beside him. "They're dead, Lieutenant." There was no ridicule in his voice, not even any particular concern. "H and E shells weigh more than

70

WP; that was explained the third day of the class. There is a correction made for it in the FDC. You should have considered this in making such radical corrections."

McCabe picked up his grids, dusted himself off, and walked slowly off the rim. Three miles away the ground was still smoking. He wasn't sure whether he felt badly because he'd killed his own men or made a stupid mistake.

The mistake on the hill had sobered him, and he began working harder. There were night fire missions, perimeter fire. It might have been interesting to use what he had learned and go to Nam as an artillery officer, but he had come into the service to acquire more than just a skill. Three days before graduation he requested airborne training, and the day artillery school was over, he went airborne.

Benning was tougher than Sill, and sharper. The men moved more quickly and looked starker. After the cerebral stuff of artillery training, the physicalness of airborne training came as an almost welcome relief. Nothing was sloppy at Benning; even the buildings seemed to have an edge on them. The first day, McCabe stood on the parade grounds and watched the groups of lean, tough troops wheeling past. The next morning he became one of them. During training there was no rank. Everyone on the field—enlisted men and officers—was treated alike. In most cases it was obvious who was who, though the instructors scrupulously ignored the obvious. The harassment never ended. They were pushed all the time.

"Those boots aren't quite right. Give me twenty."

"Sorry, but you weren't down low enough. Let's try another twenty . . . more."

"Sorry, mister, but that brass just isn't right. Go around again."

"What do you want to be? What do you want to be? Come on . . . come on . . . come on . . . come on. Go, go, go, go."

He lost ten pounds the first week. They slept four and five hours a night and then got up and ran everywhere. PT in the morning, afternoon, and evening; in groups or singly there was constant exercise. Everything—home, letters, concerns, friends—everything faded under the weight of exhaustion. "Come on, come on, come on . . . " With the few other officers he struggled along with the crazies, the tough, role-playing enlisted kids right off the streets of Chicago, Gary, and the back roads of Georgia who had gone airborne because of all the John Wayne movies they'd seen. Jump school was full of them, white and black, and among them some who were almost psychotics. There was talk at night about murders in the enlisted barracks; knifing out in the middle of nowhere; adolescent blood oaths and gang attacks. Another officer told him about a barrack race riot in the class before theirs; it had been so bloody that afterwards the MP's had to hose down the inside of the building.

"Before I got here I used to think I knew what was what," McCabe said one day as he sat using his bayonet to peel the mud off his boots. "I'll tell you something. I've talked to 'em, and they don't think they're doing anything wrong. It's their way of life, I guess. I've never lived in a ghetto."

The Shaping-Up of McCabe

"Well," his fellow officer said, "something out to be done. Ghettos or no, they're in the United States Army now."

"I don't know," McCabe said. "Maybe you have to pay a price if you want people to jump out of airplanes."

The next day they began jump training: the 34-foot tower; the 250-foot tower; water landings; tree landings; high-tension wire evasion. And for each there was that one last moment when alone he had to take that one last step. For McCabe, each last step was a struggle with fear. Each survival brought with it an increased sense of well-being, a sense of power restrained only by what had yet to be done.

There was comfort, too, in helping others and sharing and being helped himself.

Enlisted men and officers—they watched each other suit up, checked each other's gear, made sure there was nothing too sharp, nothing packed wrong. A comradeship that a few months ago McCabe would have sneered at helped to sustain him right up to the doorway of his first jump. Everyone, even the loudest and most obnoxious of the crazies, felt it. For days the tension grew. Like a wind out of the future it blew into everything they did, everything they thought. There had been injuries off the towers. Now, though, it was not simply a matter of a pulled muscle or a sprained ankle; it was a matter of dying—of falling forever.

The morning of the first jump no one ate, no one even talked. McCabe tried to shake off his fear. Like a child mumbling a lesson, he repeated to himself over and over: "I'm trained, I'm ready, I'm fit. They wouldn't send me up if they didn't think I was ready. I'm trained, I'm ready, I'm fit." He didn't care who heard him, nor did anyone care what he said. He was fighting to keep from backing out. It made everything else that had ever bothered him—exams, girls, people—seem stupid and unimportant.

Tight-lipped, their fear out in the open, they helped each other put on their gear, silently, with a solemnity that was almost suffocating. For the first time in weeks no one joked. Everyone just stood there in the barracks, strapping in his doubt, grimly getting ready. Full gear: one-hundred-and-twenty pounds of added weight. Two chutes, front and back. Equipment packs slung between their legs, weapons, webb gear, entrenching hooks, jump helmets—they strapped in their terror until, hardly able to move, they shuffled out of the barracks to the flight line. It was a hot, dazzling day, and soon every one of them was soaked with sweat. Waiting near the transports, they sat along the runway back to back, resting against each other, their hands folded nervously across the tops of their front packs. McCabe found himself trying to look at the planes through the shifting spectrum of his own sweat. He closed his eyes and tried to control his breathing.

"How you feel, man?"

"Scared."

"Me too."

"Phew!"

"Long way down—huh, man."

They had to be lifted into the planes. Sitting down, pushed together, they waited for the jump master to pull himself into the plane.

74

The Shaping-Up of McCabe

Feet braced in the doorway, the jump master was suddenly there. "Scared!" he yelled at them. There was a moment of stunned silence and then, "Airborne!" they screamed back. McCabe screamed as loud as he could. The very effort was comforting.

The jump doors slammed shut, and locked in, they began rolling jerkily down the runway. McCabe pressed his back up against the bulkhead, listening past his nervousness to the sound of the engines. The plane picked up speed, and the jerkiness increased, pitching them from side to side, like dolls on a rack. Then they were airborne. The plane lifted sharply. Even while they were climbing, the jump master unexpectedly opened the doors. Dazzled by the sudden light, they stared terrified out the open back of the plane, numbly watching the bits of cloud swirling past the open doorway. The jump master kept the door open. McCabe, despite the terror in his guts, was drawn again and again to look at the sky. He had never seen it so close, so huge.

Thirty minutes later the jump master, hanging on to the pitching plane, yelled over the noise: "Stand up!"

No one move.

"What are you?" he yelled, his face contorted with the effort. "WHAT ARE YOU?"

"AIRBORNE!" they yelled back.

"Stand up! Hook up!"

Hooking their clips into the overhead line, they pressed close together, shuffling their feet, stomping harder and harder until the whole plane was vibrating under them as they edged forward, until they were packed so tight it was difficult to breathe. McCabe rested his cheek against the pack of the trooper in front of him. As they pushed closer to the doorway he could hear the engines and the wind whistling past the opening. The jump master grabbed on to the door jambs and stuck his head out into the 120-knot wind. It tore at his face, but he remained there until he was satisfied, then turned back to the rows of stomping troopers and shouted something, but his words were lost in the wind. The plane slowed a bit as the pilot cut the inboards.

"Equipment check," he yelled over the noise.

"30-OK; 29-OK; 28-OK . . . " They were packed in so tight that when the light switched from red to green there was no place to go but out.

"Go, go, go. Go—go, go, go, go . . . " McCabe felt he was not so much moving toward the hatchway as being propelled there. The plane was bouncing now, making it tough to keep his balance. Ahead of him, they were leaping, twirling out of the doorway. "Go, go, go, go, go . . . "

Terrified, McCabe suddenly found himself even with the screaming sergeant. A great shove, and he was gone— hurtling out into the sky—a tiny brown stick twisting through all that brilliance.

Afterward he heard that the fifth time was a bit easier.

Somewhere before the end of jump school, between the third and the last jump, he decided to go on to Ranger training. There was a poster in the barracks: a tough, good-looking soldier, framed against a yellow-red background of exploding shells, grim, sleeves rolled up, an M-16 held high in one hand, a Ranger tab on his left shoulder. Across the whole thing in big block letters were the words: RANGER TRAINING MAKES A GOOD SOLDIER

The Shaping-Up of McCabe

BETTER. McCabe saw it every day. Maybe, he thought, maybe, just to do it right, he'd go, and finally two weeks before the end of jump school his decision was made. A fifth of the class went with him.

They weren't given much time between jump school and Ranger training at Fort Benning, but there wasn't much time to give. The Tet offensive had finally been stopped, and while the Army called the American defense a success of sorts, it was, even to the most myopic general, obviously a costly one. In the two months that it had taken to stop the VC, 20,000 Americans had been killed or wounded. Whole units had become inoperational. Others were running at one-half to three-fourths strength. There weren't enough first and second lieutenants to go around; sergeants were running companies, and corporals platoons.

Three days didn't even give him time to relax. Later, all he could remember about his trip home was that everything seemed so easy there, so fat, and so very dull.

"Tomorrow morning, gentlemen, we will be up at zero three-thirty. We will begin the day by running one full mile." What's all the fuss, McCabe thought; they'd run six miles at a time at airborne school.

They woke up at 3:30 in fatigues and jump boots. With forty-pound field packs on their backs, they lined up near the half-mile track of Fort Benning's jump school.

"Gentlemen," the instructor said, "we shall now run one mile—in twelve minutes." It took a moment for McCabe to realize what he was hearing. The six miles at Bragg had been a rather leisurely affair. A twelve-minute mile in full gear would almost have to be a sprint. "Tomorrow, we shall run a mile and a quarter; the day after that, a mile and a half, until you are running four miles in twenty-four minutes. Fall out!"

Everything from then on was timed—the low crawl, the parallel ladders, the run, the dodge and jump— everything. McCabe had come to Benning confident that he was in shape, but they were pushing him right from the beginning. "What's wrong, soldier, don't you want to be a Ranger?" He pushed, and still it was, "Come on, sonny, do it again." There was almost one instructor per man, and he was always there over you, pushing, shouting, yelling. Already lean, McCabe could feel himself getting leaner.

"You look a little tired, mister, want to rest?"

"Dragging there, huh? You don't want to be a Ranger, do you? Not if you move like that." Through mud and water, through the woods, carrying forty-pound ammunition cans—and each other.

"Now get your ass moving, or back to mother."

"Go back and do that again—right!"

During those first weeks at Benning, exercise became more than just PT. It took on the aspects of combat, of survival. Exhausted, they were pushed through miles of mud and water under full gear, always under full gear. They jumped blindfolded off three-meter boards, crawled for hundreds of yards, got up and did it again, and all the time they were getting less and less sleep and meeting grueling inspections. And all the time there were forced marches under full gear.

78

"The first few hours of sleep are the only ones you need. They're the deepest ones. The rest are just for dreaming. Now fall out!" They went to bed at one and two and got up at three and four. There was no heat in the barracks, and after a while it didn't matter. Everything was always done flat out—repelling down freezing cliffs, log ladders, dragging forty-pound ammunition cans through the mud, going up rocky, forty-degree slopes. An incredible numbness began to take hold of them all; McCabe drank his morning coffee while he was still in line so that he could warm his hands. Then it would begin again.

He finished drills without even remembering what he had done, pulled himself through another mile without thinking of the mile ahead. In a world removed from anything he could remember, he began losing track of days, then hours. A strange, sullen kind of rebellion began to develop. Exhausted, his humor gone, he began glaring back at the screaming instructors. Others quit; they gave up or just said "Fuck it" and went away. Rebellion would have broken out, not only with him, but with the other survivors as well; a little more pushing, another unnecessary march, just one more abuse would have done it. But just when rebellion was taking over, the instructors, as if on cue, suddenly backed off, and it was over. The troops were called out and told to get their gear together and to get into the two-and-a-half-ton trucks.

For a month they moved out, living in the cold wet foothills of Georgia. There were snug, warm Quonset huts for the instructors, but for McCabe and the others there were only poncho liners and tarpaulins. The rain, cutting through the bushes, froze on them. They woke up in the

79

morning shivering, as cold as they'd been when they'd managed to fall asleep. Moving along vague, slippery paths, they went out on patrols. Upper respiratory infections became pneumonias, pneumonias became pleurisies. The sick and the weak passed out. The rest, gulping penicillin pills, went on—pushing though the bush.

They stayed out patrolling four or five days at a time. The instructors, closemouthed and seemingly indifferent, went along but offered no help. The Georgia hills were at best difficult. In places, though, they were plainly uninhabitable, with tangles of second growth as thick as any forest anywhere. McCabe had never seen anything like it. There were times when he stood there, freezing, the rain blurring his vision, his fatigues soaked, looking into a wall of bushes and veins, with no place even to begin. They pushed through for days. Two weeks out, the patrol got lost and stayed in the field with no food for an extra thirty-one hours. When they got back, their instructor, who had been with them the entire time, failed the patrol leader and sent them out again that same afternoon.

For weeks they walked through those hills—blank-faced—with their weapons, carrying only what they needed, learning, despite the discomfort or because of it, where to put their feet, how to conserve their strength, what path to pick, how to follow a map. They got used to going for days with only ten-minute naps. There were no concessions for the weather, the land, or the men, but on night maneuvers those troopers classified as weak swimmers were allowed to put two pieces of luminescent tape on the back of their caps instead of one.

The Shaping-Up of McCabe

All the time the class grew smaller. You could quit any time. Just walk away. Once on patrol, though, all the options were gone. In a world that had once been full of possibilities there was only one left—finishing. For those who stayed, a certain pride and comradeship grew. Not the group kind at jump school, but an individual respect and reliance. There weren't enough troopers there to hold any one man up, and only one trooper could bring the whole thing down on everyone else's head. So they moved carefully through the Georgia hills, five-, six-man patrols, watching each other and learning each other's weaknesses and strengths, supporting where they could, helping if they had to.

They finished their patrolling techniques with a four-day sweep that ended up taking them into a windswept canyon where, frozen and wet, they edged themselves across slippery planks hanging sixty feet above rock-filled river beds. Two left after that, but even they had to cross the canyon to get out. McCabe felt like some kind of survivor. The future—any future—no longer seemed so worrisome.

After that last patrol the class was taken back to Benning. McCabe sat, hunched over in the back of the truck, grimly watching the hills recede. Climbing down at Benning, they were given six hours to clean up, get a steak, and get back to go to the mountains. Most went to town, but McCabe stayed by himself. He took a long, hot shower and went off to eat alone.

In the mountains, they camped high up where it was still winter, despite the fact that it was already almost April in the valleys. There were large patches of snow on the ground, and all the night temperatures were below freezing. The emphasis was not so much on working, as it was on learning the mountains. After Benning and the hills, it was almost leisurely. It was a sort of graduate school. There were field seminars on techniques, situations, execution, on administration logistics, command and signal, with the class standing around in their parkas, cradling their weapons while they listened. They learned how to repel down a cliff and advance, how to use grapples and pitons—in short, how to function in the mountains.

They learned how to pass through different kinds of danger areas, how to go through mine fields and claymores, how to cut through razor wire and dismantle trip flares. They were taught to cross any river, field, or road free or under fire, how to set up for traveling, how to camouflage. Experts were flown in from all over the States to teach them. For the first time McCabe began to feel the privilege of it all.

Self-defense gave way to infiltration and ambush. The discipline was taught just as calmly as traversing and repelling. No great emphasis was placed on these killing techniques. They were simply taught as another tool. The important thing was to get to your mission, accomplish it, and get out again.

The last week it snowed. They were on a patrol when it started—and for five days they pushed through four-foot drifts. Two boys were frostbitten, but they all finished. They returned to Benning, and after two days of briefing and lectures they went to Florida.

They were issued their jungle gear at Benning, so that when they landed at Eglin Airforce Base it was already like being deployed. They got off the planes black-faced, fully dressed and armed, and went directly from the plush, semitropical airbase into the jungle. The airmen from the base watched with amusement as they marched past. It annoyed McCabe. It annoyed them all. It was like walking through a foreign country. "Fuck 'em," he thought. "Simple bastards, simple fucken bastards."

The swamp soon undermined his pride. It was the foothills of Georgia again, only worse. They were in the jungle all the time; they patrolled in the swamps, and their base camp was in the swamps. They never got out of it. The bugs and leeches were everywhere. The men were never dry. It was incredibly hot and stinking. They slushed through the filthy water for hours, weapons at port arms to keep them dry, stopping only to pick off leeches or kill a spider. Two were bitten by snakes the first week. They slipped on sunken roots and hidden rocks, and they ate C-rations when they could, eating and drinking only what they carried.

To survive, they developed a water ecology. They learned to cut holes in their pants so that the water could drain out and how to protect each other from water bugs. The emphasis was always on the immediate. Long-range concerns and feelings were simply shoved aside or didn't matter here. An attitude of thinking began to develop: decisions couldn't be postponed; they had to be made right then and there. What to do now? What to do when this happens, and that? They were learning how to live with someone trying to kill them.

For the first time they were issued M-16's, instead of the M-14's they'd been using. They gave up their

Thompsons for the M-60's and began carrying M-79 grenade launchers. McCabe packed claymores into his rucksack and carried shotgun rounds. The instructors began to talk about killing now, and Nam was at last brought up.

"You never—I repeat, never—use a track that's already there, or come back the same way you went in. The gooks will booby-trap it for sure." The instructors put out traps for them. "Hold it, Craig. Don't move. There, by your foot." "Christ, McCabe, look out, will you? You tripped it. You'd be dead if you were in Nam."

"When you're in Nam," the instructor said, wiping the sweat off his face, "you don't jump off the track—ever. Charlie will put one sniper up on a path, fire a round, down it, and wait for you to go into the bushes and just tear yourselves apart on the punji spikes and booby traps. If anything looks wrong—rocks lying the wrong way, twigs bent—anything, remember the gooks have to let each other know where the shit is too. A piece of bamboo where it shouldn't be, wood chips, a bullet hole in a tree. They've got to know, too—remember that, and look for the signs yourself."

They set up their own ambushes: L's, V's, and X'es, and lay in the slime for hours to pull them off. They went through mock-up VC villages. They were ambushed themselves. "No, no, no. You charge toward the firing, dammit, it's your only chance. Now get the hell up and do it again." They got used to the noise of being shot at and the confusion. McCabe, twisting through the water, learned to read from the noise and the splashing of the bullets what kind of ambush it was and where the bullets were coming from.

84

"If you fall into an X-type ambush, you're just fucked," the instructor offered, kneeling down to draw an X in the mud. "Whichever way you come into it, they got you; any way you move they can light you up. If you come in through this side of the X," he said, drawing a line from the outside of the X to the place where the limbs crossed, "and you move this way"—moving the line down through the lower side of the X—"the other two limbs, just by turning around, can still have you." He looked up. "Just roll up and die, because there's nothing you can do. The L's and V's are different. If you move fast enough, you're out. Like the L," he said, wiping out the X and making an L.

They listened and then went out to practice again; it was endless. What they did well once, they did a second time, to do it better. They went on night amphibious patrols, pulling their rubber boats through the jungle tangles, launching them into the shallow water, paddling silently, cautiously, down the narrow waterways. Watching the banks as intently as if their lives depended on it, they sat in the boat, listening to the soft rippling of the water moving past them, feeling singularly alone and ageless.

The jungle training was to end with a night jump at low level into the cypress swamps of southern Florida. They were to be dropped twenty miles from the coast and were given ten days to get to the coast for an offshore amphibious pickup, followed by a water insertion farther up the coast.

The 197th Brigade stationed at Dalton and support by SF troopers were to be out in the swamps to stop them. It was understood that if the offshore pickup was missed, they would have to hump it to the second objective. It was that simple.

"Nervous?"

"Yeah, a little," McCabe said, carefully placing his C-rations into his rucksack.

"What do you think it's gonna be like? I mean, low level, in the dark. You wouldn't see anything until you hit."

"Probably as bad as we all think," McCabe said.

He sat on the flight line with the rest of them, listening to the wind whistling through the open darkness above them, hoping it would build up so the mission would be canceled. It wasn't and they jumped, black and lonely at low level, on a windy Florida night.

Just as they jumped the wind shifted, setting into them. It took Collins into a tree and broke his pelvis. It took McCabe and slammed him into the ground. He hit hard and, rolling reflexively, cut open his cheek on a rock. Before he could get up to collapse his chute, it had puffed out and dragged him through a small patch of water. Struggling, choking, trying to keep his head above the slime, he finally managed to get to his knees and cut himself loose. Disgusted, he knelt there gasping, soaked in three feet of muddy water. Forcing himself to vomit, he threw up as much of the foul liquid as he could. To drown, to die in this, he thought. Fuck it! And he left the chute unburied.

It took four hours to regroup. For five days they moved east through the swamp. Sweating, sleeves rolled up, chewing salt tablets and drinking the smelly, chemically treated water, watching, point out ahead, they sloshed through the water. Gradually the swamps thinned, the

86

water began forming itself into little creeks and then streams. They had to start rigging lifelines to get across the wider ones, and all the time they kept falling behind their schedule.

The group paused, and McCabe pointed out their position on the map. "We're here and we're late," he said. "What do you think?"

"We couldn't have keep on schedule, even without the rivers," one of the troopers said.

"That's not the point. The point is what do we do . . . ? OK," McCabe said, getting to his feet. "There's no choice."

That evening, instead of stopping, they kept on the move. Grueling days merged into grueling nights; unable to see, they followed the fluorescent tapes on the cap of the man moving in front. They switched point every hour, the front man leading the way through the blackness as best he could. Cut and bleeding, they pushed through the swamps, slipping and sliding, occasionally falling. The sixth day the point spotted an ambush; doubling back, they moved around it, but it cost them a good two hours. They just hunched over and pushed harder. Toward evening on the eighth day they finally broke out of the last of the swamps.

McCabe was point then. He was taking the patrol down a water reach, moving perpendicular to a thick, bush-lined peninsula, when he noticed something flashing in front of him.

Stopping, he held up his hand to halt the column. On his right, the reach continued around the peninsula in a kind of dog leg. He saw the flash again, and leaving the rest of the patrol motionless against the swamp line, he moved cautiously through the knee-high reeds. Nearing the bushes, he dropped his rucksack and crept forward, crawling over the roots of the cypress trees that hung onto the sandy soil. From behind the hedges he could hear light, tinkling noises. He cradled his weapon and inched forward on his hands and knees until he reached the hedge.

It took him a moment to overcome his surprise. Beyond the hedge, out in the open, a patrol—two squads and three Green Beret advisers—were setting up for dinner. They were joking and laughing as if it were a picnic.

McCabe moved silently back to the edge of the water and brought the rest of the patrol on line. He sent one half wading through the reeds off to the right; the other half he brought up through the swamps to his left.

"Don't fire until you hear my burst." McCabe crawled back to the hedge. He slipped the safety off his M-16. Unconcerned, the Green Berets were busy with their dinner; through the bushes, McCabe could hear snatches of their conversation. We must have been moving too fast, he thought; caught 'em before they had a chance to set up for us. Another few hours and it could have gone the other way. Pressing himself against the ground, he pushed the barrel of his M-16 through the tangle and settled its sights on the back of the Green Beret officer sitting in front of him, no more than six meters away. Squinting down the sights, McCabe slowly raised the barrel until the open sight was resting directly below the soldier's skull. Slowly and calmly, he pulled the trigger.

Everyone on the plain was labeled as killed. There were a few jokes, but not many. The patrol stayed just long enough to clean their weapons and take all the food they wanted, then moved off again.

They were almost to the coast now; the vegetation was thicker and more substantial, and they had to sling their weapons to fight their way through. After a half-day's march they cleared it, and they could feel the cool sea breezes blowing in from the coast. As they were moving out over some low hills a spotter plane came over, and they scrambled for cover, but no one could be sure they hadn't been seen.

"Spotter planes . . . shit!"

It would be a race now. Already brutally exhausted, they had to push even harder. The rest of the day and that night and all the next day they stopped only once for C-rations. The vegetation gave way to flat, sandy areas. Hunching up their rucksacks, they slogged on, expecting any minute to get hit. A little before midnight, too exhausted even to speak, they reached the ocean and threw themselves down on the reedy rise overlooking the shoreline and the moon-lit sea.

It was an incredibly beautiful night, cool and peaceful, with the moon lighting a broad path across the ocean that was as calm as a lake. Out at sea, silhouetted against the horizon, they could see several freighters.

"The moon's like a fucken searchlight," someone mut-tered.

Lying on the sand, McCabe swept his eyes along the moonlit coastline. As far as he could see, the beach was empty. For a moment he wondered if it would not be best to go back and find a more sheltered part of the coast.

"How long?" someone whispered.

"Three hours."

McCabe closed his eyes and rested his head on the stock of his weapon. If someone had reminded him that this was the coast of Florida, that he was at home, and that those ships out there were friendly, he wouldn't have listened—or even cared.

"When we'd go into a possible VC village and the elder said no VC, no mines, we'd say fine, and then push him along in front of us till we got out again. If he hesitated, we'd just keep pushing him till he set off the first one."

Paratrooper, 101st Airborne
Surgical Ward
U.S. Army Hospital, Kishine, Japan

6

Search
and Destroy

IT was 115 degrees in the sun, and what little shade there was offered no relief. A dull, suffocating dryness hung over the paddies, making it almost impossible to breathe. By seven-thirty, the troopers were already covered with a thin, dusty layer of salt. Instead of swallowing their salt pills, they walked along chewing them two or three at a time. A few visibly hunched their shoulders against the heat, but there was nothing to be done about it so they kept walking, trying as well as they could to shelter the metal parts of their weapons from the sun. The sweet smell of marijuana drifted along with them. A little before noon, the point man, plodding along a dusty rise, sweating under his flack vest, stepped on a pressure-detonated 105-mm shell, and for ten meters all around the road lifted itself into the air, shearing off his legs as it blew up around him. The rest of the patrol threw themselves on the ground.

That evening, the company was mortared—two rounds that sent the already exhausted troopers scurrying for shelter. After the attack, those who had been resting found it impossible to get back to sleep. The heat that the sun had poured into the Delta during the day continued to hang over them, covering them like a blanket; despite the darkness, it was still over 90 degrees. The troopers lay on the ground, smoking grass or just looking vacantly up at the empty sky. It was the fifth night that week they were hit.

Before breakfast, a patrol was sent out to sweep the area around the nearby village. The troopers got up while it was still dark, put on their webbing and flack vests, and without saying a word, went out. All they found were the usual, uncooperative villagers. The patrol, against orders, went into the village, searched a few huts, kicked in a door, and left.

Later that morning, the company began sweeping again. They moved out on line, humping through the gathering heat, chewing salt pills as they had the day before, looking out over the same shimmering landscape. A little after ten o'clock, they began moving through a hedge grove. A trooper tripped a wire and detonated a claymore set up to blow behind him. It took down three others, killing two right off and leaving the third to die later. The survivors rested around the bodies till the Dust Offs came in and took out the casualties, then started up again.

Before noon the platoon, strung out along a dike, had entered a tangled area of burned-over second growth. It wasn't so big that they couldn't have gone around, but the Old Man wanted to kill some gooks, so he sent them through it just in case. Disgusted, they moved into it, and for over two hours pushed their way through the steaming shadowy tangle. The thick overhead filtered out almost all the sunlight, making it difficult to see, while the matting of vines and bushes held onto the heat, magnifying it until the troopers felt they were moving through a breathless oven. The sweat poured off them as they moved cautiously through the suffocating half light. At places the growth was so thick that to get through they had to sling their weapons and pull the vines apart with their bare hands.

"Careful, there . . . hold it, man . . . don't move."

The vines and thorns caught onto their fatigues and

94

equipment, and they had to stop to tear themselves loose.

"Watch it, Smithy . . . hold up, Hank; there, by your foot . . ."

"Fuck . . . I'm caught."

"Watch your step, man . . ."

Scratched and bleeding, they pushed on through the tangle.

"Larry, don't move your arm. Don't move. I think I see a wire."

"It's OK, Frey. It's just a vine."

Suddenly, out on their right someone screamed.

"Don't move!" Crayson yelled. "Just don't move. I'm coming."

"Jesus Christ, I'm on one."

Pulling up short, the others froze.

Crayson and the other corporal stepped carefully through the bushes toward the trooper.

"Don't lift your foot. Freeze, man, just don't lift it."

"EOD, EOD, forward! EOD forward!"

"That fucken bastard, that fucken bastard," the trooper kept repeating, almost hysterically, "that fucken bastard," as the EOD bent down to look at the mine.

"What is it? Jesus!" he said, rigid with fear.

"It's OK," the EOD said, straightening up, wiping the sweat from his eyes. "It's pressure-release. Don't worry, it's not a bouncing betty. Just don't move."

"M-60 carriers, forward! Ammo carriers, forward!"

The EOD slipped off his rucksack, and laying down his weapon got down on his hands and knees, as the troopers came up with the boxes of M-60 ammunition.

"OK, now, just don't move," he said. "I'm gonna stack

these ammunition cans on the detonator plate. When I tell you, move your foot a bit, but don't lift it up. OK?" The EOD carefully wiped off the steel plate and placed one forty-pound can on the right side of the plate next to the trooper's foot and another on the left side of the plate.

"OK, man," the EOD said, looking up. "It's OK. Just step off."

Three-quarters of the way through the tangle, a trooper brushed against a two-inch vine, and a grenade slung at chest height went off, shattering the right side of his head and body. The medic, working down in the dim light, managed to stop the major bleeders, but could do nothing about the shattered arm and the partly destroyed skull. Nearby troopers took hold of the unconscious soldier and half carrying, half dragging him, pulled him the rest of the way through the tangle.

The platoon finally came out onto a small dirt road. Shielding their eyes from the sudden glare of sunlight, they dropped their rucksacks and sat down along the slight rise bordering the road, licking the salt off their lips as they waited for the chopper to come in and take out the body.

They were sitting there strung out along the road, when they spotted a small figure putt-putting toward them. They watched uninterestedly while the figure moved toward them, its progress marked by little puffs of grayish smoke, and became an old man driving a scooter. When the scooter was less than fifty meters away from them, the old man began to slow down.

The point, a blank-faced kid, picked up his weapon and got slowly to his feet. Holding up his hand, he walked wearily into the center of the road and stopped there, waiting. The old man slowed to a stop and stared at the trooper, waiting impatiently for him to move. He had a small steel container strapped to the back of his Honda. The point leveled his weapon at the little man's stomach and, walking around him, motioned for him to open the container. The old man hesitated. The trooper calmly clicked his M-16 to automatic. Holding it with one hand, he carefully opened the container.

"Hey," he said, lowering his weapon. "The dink's got Cokes."

The rest of the platoon got to their feet. The point was reaching into the container when the old man grabbed his wrist. Startled, the trooper jumped back.

"Hey!" He pulled his hand away. "What the fuck?"

"Fifty cent," the old man demanded, waving five fingers in the trooper's face. "Fifty cent!"

There was a moment of stunned silence.

"The little fucker steals 'em from us and then wants us to pay," someone said angrily. The point reached in again, only to have the old man slap his hand away.

"Watch it, dink," he said angrily. The Vietnamese, furious, reached for the container top and slammed it shut. From the side of the road there was the metallic click of a round being chambered. The old man turned on his scooter and kicked at the starter.

"Hold it," the corporal said, moving into the road. Others followed him and gathered around in angry, sullen silence. The Vietnamese, head down, ignoring them all, kicked again at his starter.

"I want a Coke," one of the troopers said, and swinging his rifle, he knocked the top off the steel container. The Vietnamese spun around and spit at him. The trooper took a small step backward, brought the weapon smoothly up into the crook of his arm and emptied the magazine into him, cutting him off his scooter, then calmly reached into his webbing, took out another clip, and pushed it into his gun. When the chopper came they were standing there drinking the Cokes. They sent their own dead home and left the old man sprawled in the middle of the road.

That night, a little after midnight, just as they were getting to sleep, the company was rocketed again. The first 122-mm rocket hit near their flank. The jarring whoosh of its explosion rolled over the camp, and a moment later someone was screaming for a medic.

In the morning the patrol, sweeping the area in front of the village, found the partially destroyed cross pieces of a rocket launcher. When they brought it back, the CO examined it and asked permission to hit the village. It was denied. That afternoon, two platoons of the company were ordered out of the area to take part in a combined sweep of a nearby VC stronghold. Brigade sent them some slicks, and they were CA'd in.

What was supposed to be a VC stronghold turned out to be an NVA regiment. The slicks on line brought the platoons in downwind of a little group of paddies. Even as the choppers drifted into a hover, they came under fire. While the door gunners swept the tree lines, loaches and cobras swung in and out over the LZ, shooting at anything that looked good.

The troopers, huddled in the doorways of their slicks, were being shot down before they had a chance to jump.

The air crackled with passing rounds. One of the slicks was still thirty feet off the ground when a gunship, keeping pace with them, shuddered, wavered a bit, then dropped fifteen feet and exploded, sending great pieces of metal hurtling in all directions. The 1st Platoon's six slicks brought them in closer to the tree line than the other units. Hovering three feet off the ground, the troopers jumped out into the swirling dust while the door gunners shot up the tree lines. Three troopers got hit right off, tumbling over even before they'd got their balance. Those running could hear the sledge hammer sounds of the RPD's slamming into the choppers behind them.

The second platoon was landing off to their right, the chopper's blades flattening down the bushes, while the troopers leaped out. A gunship came in low, right over the slicks, its gunner planted solidly in the door, feet braced against the struts, firing his 60 directly into the tree line. The pilot kept the chopper moving parallel to the troopers rushing the line, while the door gunner, pressing down on the trigger, kept his quad 60's cracking out in one long continuous roar. A slick exploded as it pulled out.

A cobra swept in, running down the whole length of a nearby hedgegrove, cutting it apart with its mini guns. The company charging through the heat took the wood line. Stumbling through the bushes, they overran it, killing everyone they found. Panting, barely able to catch his breath, the platoon's RTO found a wounded NVA, his shoulder and thighs smashed by the mini guns. Unable to move, he lay there, his AK broken beside him. The RTO shot him through the face.

It went on like that until the troopers had cleared the

99

line. With the gunships moving out in front they found themselves on the edge of another paddy. Beyond was a thicker tree line. The platoon's lieutenant, keeping low, moved out ahead.

"OK, OK," he said; "come on, let's go."

No one moved. The med evacs were already coming in behind them.

"Lieutenant," the Sergeant said, "they're waiting."

All along the grove, troopers were stretched out, looking grimly across the open paddy.

"I know, I know," he said, "but the gunships shook them up, and the Major wants us to go. The quicker we get at 'em the better. Don't want them to dig in."

"Shit," one of the troopers mumbled.

A machine gun opened up on their left flank.

"They've been dug in for twenty years," someone else volunteered disgustedly. "Why don't we soften the fucken thing up first."

"Let's go," the Lieutenant said flatly. "That's an order."

Bitterly they got up, and the NVA let them get halfway across the field before they hit them. They had to pull back. A gunship coming in to help was hit by an RPD, scattering itself over 200 meters of Nam. Air strikes were finally called in and then, with gunships anchoring their flanks and artillery in rolling barrages, destroying the grove and cutting off any retreat, they moved out again. Another battalion was committed and then another. In the heat of it all, more choppers, flying close support, were shot down. Finally, on the second day, what was left of the 35th NVA regiment left whatever it was they had been fighting for and simply disappeared.

Search and Destroy

That afternoon the Americans, slinging their weapons, began counting bodies. The brass flew in, and to show how pleased they were, OK'd a policy of claiming a kill for every weapon found, even without a body. The exhausted troops, eighteen- and nineteen-year old kids, ignored the congratulations and simply went on stacking the bodies, throwing them into countable piles. It was the chopper pilots, though, flying in and out of it, right through the center of an NVA regiment and losing nine choppers, who summed up the bitterness of what had happened. At dusk of that last day of fighting, they flew in a CH-47 flying crane and slung a great cargo net below it. After the counting, they helped the troopers throw the NVA bodies into the net.

They filled the net quickly, and when it was filled, the crane, blowing up great clouds of dust, rose off the flat, pock-marked paddy. When the net had cleared the ground, the crane spun slowly around its center and, carrying its dripping cargo, moved off to drop the bodies on the path of the retreating NVA.

The next morning the two platoons were flown back to the rest of their company. That first night back they were hit again—two mortar rounds. The next day on patrol near the village, the slack stepped on a buried 50-caliber bullet, driving it down on a nail and blowing off the front part of his foot. When the medic rushed to help, he tripped a pull-release bouncing betty, blowing the explosive charge up into the air. It went off behind him, the explosion and shrapnel pitching him forward onto his face. Some of the white hot metal, blowing backwards, caught the trooper coming up behind him.

The men asked to take the village, and that afternoon the company commander, fed up himself, asked Brigade for portable strobe lights so they could cordon off the village and search it at night. Brigade told him there weren't any available, so the Captain sent a squad to sweep the village before it got dark. The troopers, bitter and angry, found the village equally hostile and antagonistic. The villagers watched sullenly as the troopers, fingers on the triggers of their weapons, walked by their huts. No words were exchanged, nor any sign of recognition; the hate was palpable. Through it all the villagers had enough sense not to move; even the children stood rigidly still. Behind one of the huts, a squad found a rotting NVA medical kit. Without asking for approval they burned down the hut and waited there threateningly till it burned itself to the ground.

Half a kilometer past the village, the patrol was moving along the edge of one of the villager's paddies, trying to shield their eyes from the low-slung sun, when their point was cut down by a burst of automatic fire. Throwing themselves down, they waited for the mortars or machine-gun fire. There wasn't any, and a trooper, looking up, saw something moving away from behind the nearest hedge-grove.

"Fuck it," he screamed, the last of his adolescent control gone. In a sudden fury he ripped off his webb gear. Even before it hit the ground he was up and running. He hit the hedgegrove on a dead Iowa run, barely keeping his balance as he burst through it. The rest of the squad was running after him. Carrying their M-16's and M-79's, they raced through the line and out onto the flat behind it.

For Nam it was an incredibly abandoned affair. Helmet-less, webb gear and flack vests thrown away, these bare-headed Negro and freckle-faced kids, heads down, arms pumping, their boots barely touching the ground, ran on through the shimmering heat, stumbling over the uneven ground. Just past the next grove they caught them—a girl and two men. They caught them out in the open and killed them, shooting them down as they ran. After-wards, they stood around the sprawled bodies, chests heaving, staring in bewilderment at each other. Then they stripped the girl, cut off her nose and ears, and left her there with the other two for the villagers.

That night, a starlight scope picked up movement near the village a few minutes before three rockets hit their lager. The next morning another patrol was sent out. Half-way to the village, one of the troopers stepped on a pres-sure-release land mine. They were still close enough to carry him back to the base camp. A little before noon, a squad found three of the village water buffalo out grazing. The machine gunner set up his M-6o, carefully adjusted his sights, and while the rest of the patrol stood around him, calmly killed each buffalo in turn.

The following day a huge food cache was found buried in the area. The CO asked for a cordoning off and com-pany-size sweep of the village and surrounding area. Bri-gade sent down a lieutenant colonel. He looked at the size of the food cache, the paths leading to it from the village, listened to the stories about booby traps and in-juries, and OK'd a sweep for the next morning.

It was still dark when the men were shaken awake. "I want that fucken village locked in," the CO told the platoon leaders. "I don't want a mouse to get out, and I want every one of those huts searched. I want every floorboard pulled up, every wall knocked open. I want that village clean when we leave it. Is that understood? Clean." They filed out of the lager and waited until it was just light enough to see each other and then closed in. No one was smoking; no one said a word. There wasn't a sound except the soft footfalls of 112 troopers walking silently through the grass.

"Tet is still out there—coiling and uncoiling in the dark . . . the one truly frightening thought that can't quite be put away."

Colonel
VIP suite
U.S. Army Hospital, Zama, Japan

7

Come On! Let's Go!

A T dawn, the Australian and New Zealand soldiers fighting in Nam have a complete stand-to. They get up, all of them, while it is still dark and wait out at their perimeters, rounds chambered, until the mists burn off. The British had taught them what they learned in Malaysia and the Sudan, from Omdurman and Ismalia, that if you're attacked the attack will probably come out of the darkness. So they get ready.

We don't. Perhaps it is command laziness or just plain American pragmatism of not wanting to be bothered unless there is something to show for it. Whatever the reason, we stay asleep, and the dawn for us belongs to the few scattered perimeter guards, the razor wire, and the cooks. Most of the time it works.

"Wake up, come on, James, get your ass moving . . . come on!"

Turning over, James shook off the Sergeant's hand.

"Come on."

"OK, OK!" he said angrily, pulling the wet poncho liner up over his head.

"Come on! Let's go!"

"OK, OK, OK!" James pulled the liner even tighter around his head. He lay there till he was sure the Sergeant had gone and then turning over again, pulled his arm out from under the poncho. Holding his hand close to his face, he could barely make out the luminescent dials of his watch.

"Shit!" Sighing, he let his hand drop wearily back to his side. He lay there a moment longer and then, shiver-

ing, sat up and kicked off his liner. He could hear the
Sergeant moving around in the dark, waking the other
cooks. At three-thirty in the morning the top of the jungle
is just becoming visible. The skies are lightening, but the
ground mists, heavy and sullen, snuff out what little light
there is, making it almost impossible to see even a few
meters. He began lacing up his boots. Suddenly there was
a noise, a short distant sound, muffled by the heavy air. He
froze. Now a second, closer this time, more metallic. The
others the Sergeant had wakened stopped moving.
Cautiously, James reached across his flack vest for his
rifle.

"It's OK," someone whispered. "Just the guards."

Relaxing, he let go of his rifle and finished lacing up his
boots. Across the perimeter an icy blue flame flickered,
hesitated a moment, and then catching, burned cheerlessly
against the firm grayness of the fire base. A second one
caught near it and then a third. Figures like ghosts floated
back and forth in front of the flames.

By the time James reached the mess area all the gas
burners had been lit, and the Sergeant was already stacking empty crates for the food line. A few strips of corru-
gated aluminum siding stretched over the open burners
were being heated for a grill. Two troopers, barely visible
in the dim light, were filling the fifty-five-gallon cans with
water for coffee.

"James," the Sergeant said, "we've got three dozen
fresh eggs over there by the ammunition. Mix 'em with
the powder."

"Where?"

"There, dammit," the Sergeant said, pointing. "Over

108

there near the 50's. Kolstein!" he yelled, "get some more water into those cans."

"Toast?" James asked.

"Toast what?"

"Are we going to have toast?"

"Maybe you want some caviar," the Sergeant said.

"It would be a nice morning for toast. . . . OK, forget it."

It was getting lighter. He took a few steps out over the uneven ground, stopped, and turned around.

"Any bacon?"

"You getting wise again," the Sergeant said angrily. "I've warned you."

James shrugged and continued on his way. The eggs were piled behind the 50-caliber ammunition. He never found them. The first round hit in the middle of the ammunition.

It was the same all over Nam. During Tet and the following seven weeks 4114 Americans were killed, 19,285 were wounded, and 604 were lost. But on that morning, it was the cooks and the perimeter guards who died first. At the 101st base camp near Bien Hoa there is still hanging over the rifle range a great enameled screaming eagle and above it, in twelve-inch block letters, the motto: "WE AIM TO KILL." Beneath it is this proud little commemoration:

THE ONLY U.S. RIFLE RANGE OCCUPIED BY ENEMY TROOPS DURING THE TET OFFENSIVE. FORTY - EIGHT KILLED DOWN RANGE—AIRBORNE.

"Don't let the news media fool you. These
kids may be eighteen or nineteen,
but they're beautiful killers—just beautiful."

Major, 25th Division
Medical Ward
U.S. Army Hospital, Zama, Japan

8

No Fucken Cornflakes

THERE were no more heavily armed night patrols setting up outside the perimeter of the fire base and shooting up anything that came near. The gooks would fix their position, set up an ambush, and get them coming back in the morning. Then Brigade had tried roving patrols, but the troopers, untrained for night action, got themselves caught and murdered out in the open. There was talk about giving up the whole idea and leaving Charlie everything outside the NPD, but the Old Man wouldn't have it. So they asked for volunteers—eighteen- and nineteen-year-olds—two-man ambush teams who would crawl out at night and bring down anything they could. No guns, no webb gear or helmet or even a canteen —nothing that could make any noise and give them away. The thing was to go out clean, with only a knife or a bayonet—and maybe a bicycle chain.

"Ready?" Cram asked.

Johnson held the mirror closer as he blackened the last exposed patch of his right cheek. It was almost dusk; the perimeter guards were already moving out toward the wire.

"Come on, come on," Cram said, nervously tapping his hunting knife against his thigh, while Johnson tilted the mirror to take advantage of the fading light for a final check on his face.

"Jesus, man, come on, will you?"

"OK, OK," Johnson said, dropping the mirror into his rucksack. Two of the guards, their M-60's casually slung behind their shoulders, stared at them as they passed. Johnson waved to them.

"For Christ's sake," Cram said, "you can wave at the crowd when we get back."

Johnson walked over to one of the scattered ammunition crates and, resting his foot on it, tightened the bayonet sheath strapped to his leg. Straightening up, he shook his foot and stamped on the ground to make sure the bayonet was securely clipped in its scabbard.

"The wire," he said. "Whose idea was it?"

"How the hell should I know?" Cram said.

"It ain't a good idea. It wouldn't keep 'em out, and if they hit us, it's gonna keep us in."

"Well, Mr. Strategist, since we ain't gonna be inside, we don't have to worry about that now, do we?"

"It's still a piss-poor idea."

"Tell the Old Man tomorrow, will you?"

Johnson shrugged as he squinted into the last bit of the sun. "What we got?" he asked.

"Northwest, 180 to 270 degrees. The C and C chopper saw a few of 'em moving in late this afternoon. They lit up a couple. Figured the rest got away."

"Want one?" Johnson pointed toward the ammunition crate. "Still some grenades in there."

"Look, man, you know we're not supposed to," Cram said.

Johnson reached into the crate anyway. "Sure?"

"Listen, wise guy, just because this is your second time . . ."

"OK," Johnson said, dropping the grenade back into the box.

"Got your chain?"

"Yeah."

"Let's go."

As they walked across the uneven ground toward the perimeter, Cram scanned the tree line bordering the wire.

"Hold it," he said, pulling up short.

"What the hell's burning your ass now?" Johnson said.

"That." Cram pointed to his companion's shoulder patch.

"Oh, for Christ's sake. They can't see it in the dark."

"It's yellow."

"So's the fucken leaves."

"Leaves don't move."

"You win," Johnson said, tearing the patch off his tiger stripes. "Just wanted 'em to know who the hell we were."

"They know, man," Cram said. "Just cool it a while, huh?"

They walked on past the last of the tents, toward where the guards were digging in behind the wire. About fifty meters from the perimeter they stopped and in the dim light carefully checked each other's clothing to make sure nothing could catch or was loose enough to jingle.

"Got it taped?" Cram said.

"Sure."

"Let's see it."

"I told you, it's taped."

"Let's just see it, huh?"

Johnson took out his bicycle chain and held it up for Cram to see. Each steel link was covered with strips of black heavy-duty mechanic's tape.

"Satisfied? It's tough, man, don't worry."

It was almost dark by the time they reached the wire. The weapons were already set up, and the guards were trying to make themselves comfortable.

Cram got down on his belly and crawled under the wire. Johnson followed. The ground was still soft from the rains. With the last bit of daylight fading, they crawled single file through the claymores, out past the trip flares and the phosphorous grenades, and into the high grass. About 150 meters beyond the last claymore, Cram paused to wait for Johnson, then rolled over on his side, took a ball of twine from his pocket, and looped one end of the twine around his wrist and the other around Johnson's. Tying the last knot, he tapped Johnson playfully on his bush hat, rolled back on his stomach, and began crawling again. Fifteen minutes later they came to a burned-over second growth of low bushes and grass.

"Here?" Johnson whispered.

"OK."

They sat up back to back, each taking the 180 degrees in front of him. Resting quietly against each other, their legs drawn up in front of them, they sat listening as they scanned the tips of the barely visible grass and bushes that hid them, adjusting their breathing to the night sounds around them, quieting with every sudden noise, and holding their breath with each unexpected silence. A mortar thudded in the distance; a bird screeched; a mosquito hummed close by. Far away they could hear the sound of automatic fire.

Cram turned his head. Johnson tensed; he had heard it at the same time, off to the right and a little in front of them. It was followed by a second noise, a sharp snapping, then another.

"Buffalo?" Johnson whispered nervously.

Cram was straining to hear. "No. Let's go."

Crawling on their stomachs again, they moved off the rise, parallel to the direction of the noise. Side by side, they snaked their way back into the tangle on their hands and knees, stopping every three or four meters to listen. The sounds were getting louder, the crunching, soft, measured beat of men pushing through the jungle. Cram tugged on the twine and Johnson moved off with him, perpendicular to the way they'd been going, until suddenly it was ominously quiet.

The two boys froze. To their right they heard the sharp metallic click of a round being chambered. Johnson, his heart pounding through his head, closed his eyes, straining to hear beyond his own breathing.

The first gook broke out a little to Cram's left—a dark shape silhouetted against the darker night—and as abruptly faded from view. Only the shadowy, swaying bushes showed someone had been there. Then silence again, and the night closing in on them again.

Suddenly another form appeared. The figure seemed to hesitate and was about to turn back when Cram leaped up and got him. For a moment, as Cram worked in his knife, it looked as if they were embracing, then quietly Cram lowered the body to the ground.

Johnson was still crouched when the grass next to him parted. He saw a foot, and twisting up, swung his bicycle chain in a long vicious arc. The gook was just bringing up his AK when the chain caught him across the face. Even as he fell backwards Johnson was on him, his fingers digging into what was left of the man's face. As they thudded to the ground, Johnson reached frantically for his bayonet and plunged it into the man's neck, knifing again and again until he could feel the head coming loose in his other hand —until, exhausted, he collapsed beside his victim, gasping for air with his mouth wide open to smother the sound of his labored breathing.

Terrified, he looked around. No one was coming. He sat up and felt along the ground for his chain. His hand brushed against a rifle. Picking up the AK he held it in one hand while he searched for the chain with the other, then went back to the body. He pulled his bayonet from the dead man's neck and a gush of blood flowed out with it. Johnson stared at his stained fingers; in the dim moonlight the blood looked like quicksilver. The tug at his wrist brought him back, and in another moment Cram was beside him.

"Come on," Cram whispered. "They might be coming back . . . . Hey! Leave it."

"Huh?" Johnson slipped the bayonet back into its scabbard.

"Leave it. The rifle, man. Leave it."

"Nothing doing," Johnson shook his head. "This one I'm keeping."

"Why the hell don't you just cut off an ear? Anyway, don't use it, or you'll have the gooks and our whole goddamn division trying to light us up."

Johnson slung the weapon across his back and, tightening the cinch to hold it firm, followed Cram. They crawled for almost a hundred meters before they stopped to rest again and wait for daylight—or more victims.

Toward morning a gunship circled over them. They could hear it crisscrossing above them.

"Think they've seen us?" Cram asked nervously. "I mean, maybe they'll think we're VC."

"Could be," Johnson said quietly, rubbing the wooden stock of the AK.

Cram grunted. "Must be how the gooks feel."

There was nothing to do but wait out what was left of the night until the mists burned off. When it was light enough to see clearly, they started moving back to the base.

The perimeter guards were dismantling their night positions. They looked curiously at the two boys coming through the high grass. They reached the wire a little after five. The sun had only been up an hour, but already they were soaked with sweat. Nam is at best a nervous place; there's no time for the foolishness of passwords or cricket clicks, so you wait until you can be seen. Following Cram, Johnson crawled in under the wire, the same way they had gone out the night before.

"Where's your souvenir?" someone yelled.

"Left him out there," Cram called back good-naturedly.

The base was already on the move. All around them troopers were getting ready for their morning sweeps. A few stood by their tents. Some were filling their canteens, others fixing their webb gear, hooking on grenades and smoke bombs or adjusting belts of machine-gun ammunition.

Cram put his fingers to his lips and let out a long piercing whistle. Everyone around them jumped.

"Crazy fuckers," a trooper said disgustedly, slamming a clip into his grenade launcher. "All these ambushers are fucken crazy."

119

Ahead of them, two troopers in tiger suits, one Negro and one black-faced, had turned around at the sound of the whistle. They waited for Cram and Johnson to catch up with them.

"Got one, huh?" the Negro said, looking at Johnson's AK.

"One apiece," Cram said.

"Come on, I'm hungry," the white guy said. "Let's go eat."

The four walked together the rest of the way to the mess tent. It was almost in the center of the fire base, close to the C and C. Two other ambush teams were already there, waiting in line. One trooper had a steel-tipped blackjack hanging down from a lanyard tied to his wrist. Another, a big rawboned southern boy, was playing with a barber's razor, mechanically opening and shutting the blade. They were all filthy.

"Hey, Thompson, where's Zim?" Cram asked.

"The gooks got him," the southerner said. "We're going out after breakfast to get him. The Old Man said it would be OK."

"And Cockrane?"

"He got back, but he took a round through his shoulder."

Johnson put his AK down against one of the tent supports and got in line behind the Negro.

"How did it go, Williams?"

"A bit heavy."

"Yeah," Johnson said, "for us too."

The first few guys in line began moving into the tent, and a trooper with a soiled blue bandana wrapped around his head got into line next to Johnson.

"How did you get it, man?" he said, nodding toward the AK.

"Bicycle chain."

"Worked, huh?"

"I swear, Truex," Johnson said, "he would have had me. I mean I couldn't have got to him without it. You know, I mean he would have blasted me."

"That you?" Truex asked, pointing down at Johnson's bloody hand.

Johnson looked thoughtfully at his hand. He seemed suddenly subdued, almost awed. "No," he said, "that's him."

"Yeah, I know. I got some of mine on me, too," Truex said. "Took him down from behind. Must have got an artery right off. Jesus! I mean I even got some in my mouth."

"Hey, Truex," a passing soldier yelled. "There's a letter for you in your tent."

"From who?" the trooper yelled back.

"Miss America—who the fuck else do you think?"

"Wise ass," Truex muttered to himself as he moved into the tent. Johnson followed him.

The tent sheltered them from the sun, but afforded little comfort. Hot, suffocating breezes blew unhindered straight through the open slats. Sweating, the men picked up their trays. Ahead of them, Cram stopped to pour himself some hot coffee.

"You crazy!" Williams said.

Cram looked over his shoulder at the Negro trooper. "You're supposed to drink hot things in hot weather."

"Who the fuck told you that?"

"Our family doctor, and he's a lot smarter than you are."

The Negro turned his head to watch a squad of troopers walking past the tent.

"Hey, Thompson," Truex said, "why don't they ever let us capture some prisoners?"

The southerner ignored him.

"No man, I mean it."

"What the fuck you gonna do with 'em?" Thompson asked.

"What do you mean?"

"What, I said. What the hell are you gonna do with 'em? Watch 'em all night?"

"You don't have to kill 'em to keep 'em quiet. I mean, you can tie 'em up, or keep hitting 'em on the head."

"You keep hitting them on the head," Thompson said disgustedly.

Truex shrugged. "I gotta take a piss," he announced, and left the line.

Thompson watched him duck under the tent beam and walk out into the sunlight. "That fucker's gonna kill me," he said angrily.

"How you figure that?" Williams said.

"He's gonna kill himself and me with him. We went out last night really far; I mean it was really far. He killed one going out—some kid—no weapons, nothing. Probably just from one of the villages. Anyway, the crum got pissed. He wanted an NVA. Stupid fucker."

"Why?"

"Motherfucker wants enough NVA belt buckles for a chain. Ever since he killed that NVA three days ago he's been goofy about it. That's all he talks about, getting that fucken chain. Anyway, that kid he lit up must have been something special to somebody. They were out looking for him all night. Must have been a goddamn company out hunting for him. We laid low. About midnight they were moving back past us. Every fucken one of them had gone by when I swear to god that son of a bitch Truex coughed. I swear to god, that son of a bitch coughed to get some of 'em to come back."

"Did they?" Johnson asked.

"Fucken A they did, right at us. At least they started. I had some grenades and I just threw 'em as far as I could and got the hell out in a hurry."

"And Truex?"

"He sat there like he had a string of claymores. I just cut out on him."

"Maybe you ought to tell the Old Man," Williams said.

"I'm just gonna tell Truex," Thompson said grimly.

"What time we going out for Zim?" Johnson asked as they moved onto the food line.

"I'd thought we'd go out a bit early tonight and get him," Williams said.

"Yeah, and they'll be waiting for us," Johnson said. "Why not now? It shouldn't take long to find him, and with the choppers flying around, the gooks'll be keeping their heads down."

"Oh, shit!" Cram yelled so loudly, so suddenly, that everyone stopped talking. "They're out of corn flakes. Hey, you!" he called to the cook at the back of the tent. "You're out of fucken corn flakes. Yeah, you, goddammit! Where the hell are the corn flakes?"

The cook didn't bother to answer. He just turned his thumbs down.

"Fuck it!" Cram yelled, slamming his hand down on the counter. "We work all night; you'd think they'd keep some fucken corn flakes for us. Motherfuckers! Fucken greedy motherfuckers!"

"Tracks make so much noise everyone
knows you're coming."

Trooper, 25th Division
Surgical Ward
U.S. Army Hospital, Zama, Japan

9

Track Unit

DENNEN was geared for war. After taking all the infantry and airborne training the Army could give him, he was assigned to a mechanized battalion of the 25th Division. Two days after he got to Nam he was choppered to his unit.

Dennen sat next to the crew chief the whole way out, looking over the M-60 machine gun at the checkerboard landscape rushing beneath them. He was checking the bolt on his M-16 when the crew chief tapped him on the shoulder and pointed out the open doorway. For a moment, Dennen couldn't see anything. Then against the dark green of a tree line, he saw something flash. A moment later there was another flash, followed by a puff of white smoke.

"Phantoms," the crew chief said, yelling over the rumbling of the chopper's engines. Dennen, watching the smoke clear, slid home the bolt. Against all that green the puff of smoke looked insignificant.

The headquarters for the 25th Division lay forty miles northwest of Saigon, in the foothills of the central highlands. The Army had placed it astride one of the major infiltration routes from Cambodia; part of the protective arc offered up to Saigon by the 9th Division in the Delta, the 25th, based on Cu Chi, and the American and the 1st Division farther north. During the dry season, the land the 25th worked reached from impenetrable jungle, triple canopied, in the west to rice paddies in the south and north. During the monsoons, the jungle became wet and the paddies impassable, but it was dry now; the jungle was burning off and the paddies were rock-hard.

The chopper stayed at 1500 feet, out of the range of small arms fire, until it was over the base camp. Dennen braced himself as the pilot auto-rotated the copter down, and the huge base swung up at him. From 1500 feet it had looked like a great open dump, but as they plunged down, it became thousands of khaki-colored vehicles, fuel tanks and bunkers, and finally, as they came in, drab green Quonset huts. At the last moment the pilot eased up and, lowering the chopper down past a building, set it to rest on the pad.

The crew chief slid the machine gun along its mounting so that Dennen could get out the door. Bent over, carrying his duffel bag, he walked out from under the blades. The pilot, his head out the window, waited for him to clear the rotors, then gunning the engine, he nudged the chopper off the ground and, swinging it far out to the left, pulled it off the pad. In the three minutes it took Dennen to walk to the personnel center he was completely soaked with sweat.

Headquarters was sandbagged up to the windows. MP's guarded all the entrances; it was all very proper and very military. Dennen was taken to Major Cohen, the personnel officer. The Major welcomed him to the unit, looked over his record, and going over to the map, showed him where they were and where he'd be. Dennen was about to leave when Cohen stopped him.

"Lieutenant."

"Yes, sir," Dennen said stiffly, coming to attention as he turned around.

"I see you're a Ranger."

"Yes, sir."

"Tracks are different than what you're used to; they're noisy. You can hear 'em coming. I want at least one gook for every track we lose."

"Yes, sir."

"Good luck, Lieutenant."

That evening Dennen rode out to his unit on a supply chopper carrying new machine gun barrels. The company had been fighting all day and had burned out almost all their 50's. Still taking sporadic fire, they'd pulled into a night perimeter and needed the barrels in case they got hit again that night.

"They're kicking some ass out there, sir," the chopper pilot said. "It might be hot. We could get you out in the morning."

"Will it be any better in the morning?" Dennen asked.

"No, probably not."

"I'll go, now."

"OK," the pilot said, "then would you mind . . ."

Dennen helped them load up. They took rolls of razor wire, crates of ammunition, medical supplies, and cans of water, loading the chopper until it was full. It was almost dark before Dennen, with his weapon resting between his feet, settled in beside the door gunner.

"Could be bad news," the gunner said, handing him a radio helmet. "Night ain't the best time to go in hot."

The pilot revved the engine and, pulling a little pitch, lifted the craft. It moved forward a few yards, only to settle down again. The pilot gave it more rpm's, and the chopper lifted straining, lifted again, and settled back onto the pad.

"Overloaded," the crew chief yelled.

Adding power, the pilot gunned the engine, bouncing the chopper down the runway to substitute forward speed for lift. He continued to push the engine, making the chopper vibrate so violently that Dennen could hardly keep his feet in one spot. As the helicopter gained height, the jolts became harder and harder and farther apart until finally halfway down the runway it stayed airborne. The door gunner, puffing out his cheeks in relief, sat down on one of the ammunition crates.

The pilot quickly took the chopper up to 1500 feet and turned northwest. The gunner plugged Dennen's head set into the overhead radio jack. Outside the chopper, it was dark. Dennen could barely make out the edge of the horizon. A few stars were just becoming visible. Suddenly, ten minutes out, sharp cracking sounds began snapping past the open doorway. The pilot suddenly dropped the chopper and slid it off to the left. As they fell, Dennen could see a thin bluish-green line arching up at them out of the blackness.

"Watch that son of a bitch," the pilot said over the intercom. Wrenching the chopper around, he took it back to the right.

"Four o'clock," the gunner said, looking out the open doorway.

"Going down!" the pilot's voice crackled through the head set.

Another burst of greenish-blue light hurtled past the open side of the chopper.

"Watch out, Ralph."

"Roger that."

Dennen moved back to give the gunner room to swing his M-60. Diving, the tracers followed them down to almost 500 feet and then stopped. The pilot leveled off.

Holding onto the door struts, Dennen looked at the gunner, who was grinning as he held up his thumb. The pilot's voice cut into the radio set. "36, this is 33 Spider. Approximately 05 out from location. Please mark the LZ."

"33 Spider, this is 36. Roger that."

"36, this is 33. Are you taking fire?"

"33, roger that."

"36, this is 33. What kind?"

"33," the voice, strained and tired, came through Dennen's head set. "Mortars; repeat, mortars. Will mark with strobe."

"36, this is 33. Roger that. Will come right in."

"33, affirmative."

A few minutes later Dennen could see ahead of them a brilliant sharp white light flickering in the center of miles of blackness.

"36, this is 33 Spider. I have strobe in sight."

"33, roger that."

The pilot banked the chopper toward the light and flew in over the perimeter defense. Dennen watched the darkened silhouettes of tanks and armored personnel carriers pass under them. The pilot was easing into a hover when the gunner slapped his hands to his face, jerked upright, and fell backwards onto the shell cases behind him. Dennen grabbed him as he began sliding down the cases. Blood, turned a strange metallic green by the flashing strobe, ran out from under the gunner's

131

helmet. Dennen ripped it off. The whole back of the boy's head was gone—blown away. Dennen held him till the chopper landed.

In the dark they took the body from him. The first sergeant, a grenade launcher tucked into the crook of his arm, led the way to the Old Man.

It was difficult going. The tracks had flattened the jungle but not destroyed it. The roots and veins were still there, bent and broken, all over the ground. They stumbled through to the center of the base, which was surrounded by tracks—thirty- and forty-ton shadows facing out in a circular perimeter defense with the command track, fire track, and angel track in the center.

The troopers not on guard duty stood huddled up against their machines. No one was smoking. There were no lights. Dennen and the Sergeant had almost reached the command track when one of the 50's off to their right began opening up. A moment later, an RPG sputtered across the perimeter. Everyone hit the ground while that whole quadrant of the perimeter began firing. The noise was deafening. Kneeling, Dennen tried to see where the fire was coming from. Beside him the Sergeant broke open his grenade launcher and slipped in a round. Suddenly one of the tracks exploded. There was a hissing roar as the gasoline went off and a towering flame lit the whole area. Dennen could see figures hunched over, running from the fire, as the sharp firing of the AK's broke over them.

Dennen got to his feet. "Get that tank over there," he shouted. Mortars began whooshing into the perimeter. Silhouetted against the flames, troopers could be seen tumbling over as they were hit.

"Get it going, goddammit," Dennen yelled. "Get that tank over there." A sniper round whistled by his head. "That tank! Yes, you, move it out . . . . Now, dammit . . . . There!"

Roaring and puffing, the tank began backing up. From all sides of the perimeter red tracers sliced out into the surrounding jungle.

Dennen, urgently motioning the tank on, stepped out of the way as it rolled by. Gaining speed, it hit the burning track at almost twenty miles an hour, rolling it over into the jungle. With a grinding of metal it pushed the flaming wreck out of the perimeter and into the ground, putting out the fire. There, with tracer rounds skipping off its armor plate, the tank shifted gears and, with its machine guns roaring, began moving back into the perimeter. Dennen gathered some troopers and, moving out toward it, they killed three VC who were following it in. The incoming rounds stopped. The Sergeant found him again setting up a new perimeter.

"Sorry, sir," he said, "it ain't always like this."

"There any patrols out?"

"No, sir, just our perimeter defenses."

"There should have been!"

The ground was a shambles. All around them, in the suffocating dark night, medics were working on the wounded while the RTO's were using the radios to call in Dust Offs.

They found the Captain near his command track, but in the dark Dennen could barely make out his face; the light from the radio dials was the only illumination.

The Captain motioned for Dennen to wait while he finished calling for gunships. Dennen leaned against the track, holding his M-16 in his arms. He counted two tanks and eleven APC's; counting the one that had burned, that would be twelve. Each APC, he figured, carried one 50 and two M-60's. At 1500 rounds per minute, that was a lot of fire power. Add the tracks together, and the amount became enormous. It would take a battalion even to hope to overrun their perimeter.

"Water, sir," one of the troopers said, handing him a cup.

"Yeah, thanks. Where did you get it?"

"From the track."

Dennen shook his head. "How many gallons does each track carry?" He could remember making it a day and a half on two canteens.

"About fifty."

"Plush," Dennen said, handing back the cup. Well, he thought, at least he'd be moving in comfort.

The Captain put down the horn.

"Not the best night to arrive," he said almost apologetically.

"What is it? I mean, what did you run into?" Dennen took off his helmet and wiped his forehead.

"I don't know," the Captain said wearily. "Must be a base camp, I guess. They've been fighting us every goddamn inch of the way. We're close to something, or they'd have pulled out. I lost two tracks today—three." He pointed to the wreck still smoldering in the jungle. "Whatever it is, they don't want to give it up. They'll fight when they've caught us, or when they don't want to give something up. Anyway," he said, "I'm glad you're here. Our forward observer was hit two days ago. You'll be with the second platoon. I have the third and Sergeant Smith the first. First time with tracks?"

"Yes, sir, first time," Dennen said. "I was infantry and Airborne."

"Well, try to get some sleep. I think they'll leave us alone for a while. Smith, take him to his track."

A short time later, the gunships came over.

The Dust Offs flew in and out all night. Kept awake, Dennen listened to them moving in and out over his head. The noise was appalling. He had never heard such sustained racket. If the gooks weren't awake before, they surely were now.

Dennen was pleased at how calm he'd been—his first firefight. He'd been ready. They'd made him ready—the months of training, the time in Florida, jump school. He lay there listening to the movement around him, comforted in the knowledge that he was as well trained as any soldier anywhere.

For Dennen there was nothing unnatural in what had happened. Fighting, for him, was a part of living. The strong won out, and the weak went under. That was all there was to it. Of course there was suffering, but that was the price you paid.

At daybreak the boys, wearing their flack jackets and steel pots, sat on their tracks, eating breakfast, while the Captain met with the unit Commanders. He had the map spread out in front of his track.

"OK," he said, pointing down at the map. "We'll go through in column. I want the two big boys leading the first and third platoons. I'll take the center. When we hit something big, spread out in line and pull back 250

135

meters and let the gunships and artillery handle it. If it's big, Brigade will CA in some legs. Dennen," he added, "if it is big, I want you to put the arty in about 500 meters behind their position. I'll call in gunships to anchor the flanks, and we'll drive them into the arty."

Dennen's platoon took the first column. Settling into the command seat behind the 50, he motioned them forward, taking his APC to a position behind the lead tank.

It was not yet six o'clock when they began crashing through the jungle. He had never seen anything like it, even in Florida. It was like moving through a thick live curtain. Everything was circular and growing from the top down rather than the bottom up. Great vines—millions of them—some two or three inches thick, intertwined with one another, were anchored to roots crawling along the ground. Shrubs, some the height of small bushes, hid the roots under their tubular branches. Bamboo-like plants, five or six feet tall, shot up straight as poles through the tangle, cutting out what little sun got through the vines.

Bouncing and jumping, the tracks tore their way through this tangle, with the 56-ton tank in the lead to level a path. The three columns had to stay within ten feet of each other to keep visual contact, and even then they lost each other for minutes on end. The noise was always there, and over the smell of rotting plants was the thick nauseating odor of hot oil and gasoline.

They had been moving for half an hour when an APC in the column off to Dennen's right suddenly spun to its left and began crashing through the bushes toward them, only to stop as suddenly, tilted, with its front end in a ditch.

"31/8," the radio in front of Dennen blasted out, "31/8 threw a tread."

"31/8," the radio crackled again, "how long will it take to repair?"

Dennen stopped his column.

"31/8, about an hour."

"44/8, 43, and 32 stay with 31. Catch up when fixed."

Dennen pulled his APC out of the line and pushed through the jungle toward the damaged track. The three support tracks, turning out of their columns, joined Dennen's APC in a diamond formation around the disabled vehicle, swinging out their weapons to cover all the flanks. Dennen ordered one gunner to stay on top of each track and the rest to stay on the ground. It was grueling, heavy work repairing the disabled vehicle. Guarded by their own tracks, the men strained to remove the heavy links. Far away they could hear the sound of explosions muffled by the jungle. Dennen, stripped to the waist and struggling with the jack stopped to listen.

"Grenades," one of the troopers said. "The gooks string wires along the trees and hang grenades on them with the pin almost out. The track's antennas catch the wires, pulling the grenades out of the trees, and bang! Most of the time they get everybody riding on top."

"Sometimes they hang some phosphorous," another trooper said. "That really kicks some ass."

When the tank was fixed, they pulled out. Dennen ignored the path made by the tanks that had gone ahead and pulled his column off almost 100 meters before he turned in the direction the company had gone. He caught up with them about an hour later, and for the rest of the morning the whole unit drove back and forth across their sector.

At noon they lost another APC. It was like a ship being suddenly torpedoed. One moment it was there, riding in column, bold and brassy, and the next it was broken and burning, its insides blown out. The gunners on the other tracks swept their guns from side to side, and the troopers riding on the APC's took the safeties off their weapons.

Dennen stopped his column and, sliding off his APC, walked over to the burning track. The gunners had been thrown clear; the medic was already bent over one of them. The track was lying on its side and above the tread was a small hole no more than four inches across. The steel around it was smoldering red. Dennen called over Sergeant Smith, and the two of them walked back to the place where the track had been hit.

"The rocket went in like this," Dennen said, holding his arm up at a thirty-degree angle. "It must have hit right here, where the tracks spun. So the rocket," he said, looking behind him, "must have come from over there." Switching his weapon to automatic, he walked with the Sergeant off the path into the jungle. After a few minutes of searching, they found a tunnel. The whole area was covered with them.

"That's the way it is, Lieutenant," the Sergeant said. "They've had twenty years of making tunnels—all over the area—all over Nam, I guess. Sometimes the tunnels go down deep; sometimes they're near the surface. When they get near the surface like this one, they run them parallel to where they think we might be going. All you have to do then is punch a hole out of the side, lie there with your RPG, and when a track comes by or a squad, bamb! A second later they're gone. No need to police up any brace. Gives 'em the jump, don't it?"

"Yeah," Dennen said. "But sometimes, we find them out in the open and in a sit-down drag-out, we've got them every time."

They found nothing that day, just a few bunkers. That night they got hit again. Dennen called a few rounds of artillery into the area he thought the mortars might be coming from, and that seemed to be it for the night.

The next day they moved farther west. The jungle was a furnace; at times it hit 120 degrees. If it hadn't been for the shade, the tracks would have been too hot to touch. The men rode in their T-shirts, slumped over their guns. It was too hot to talk. Even with twenty or thirty salt pills a day some of the troopers collapsed.

That day they found an arms cache and blew it up. Ten replacements came in at night. Dennen sent in pre-arranged coordinates so he'd be able to call in the artillery right on the deck even in the dark. They took two rounds that night, and Dennen quickly sent ten salvos of H and E into the area. In the morning they found ten dead gooks sprawled among the 105-mm-shell craters.

The next day a loach, flying observation, reported a lot of movement about six kilometers from where they lagered. The loach was shot down and the first APC was hit about a kilometer from the area. A tank was hit a short time later.

A spotter plane reported what looked like a big NVA camp, and the columns pushed toward it. Through the jungle the lead tanks reported figures moving, and soon the gooks broke from cover on their flanks. Dennen emptied his magazine as his gunners were swinging around their 50's. Two figures collapsed. There was a roar as the RPD's opened up, and the 50's and M-60's began firing back, slicing rounds into the surrounding jungle. A grenade bounced off a track and exploded, fragging the gunner; the other gunner swung his 60 around and cut down the gook who'd thrown it. The moaning of the nearly dead trooper was smothered by an RPG that came whistling in. Hitting the dirt, it buried itself before it went off, throwing a cloud of dirt and flame up into the air. All along the column the machine guns were roaring.

Dennen slammed another clip into the nearest clump of trees. A trooper behind him suddenly pushed him down and threw a grenade out over his head into the bushes. More grenades followed.

"We're into it," the trooper yelled, jumping off the track and firing his M-79 as he hit the ground. Bullets skidded off the armor plate of the APC. Dennen saw a trooper cut down three VC no more than five feet away from him.

A cobra, roaring down, ran the length of the column.

"Pull back, pull back," the radio squawked.

The column, still firing, picked up their wounded and, draping them across their armor, backed off, leaving the disabled tracks where they stood. Then they regrouped and spread themselves out in line, forming a half arc with every gun firing. A hundred meters of continuous automatic fire cut down the surrounding jungle as if it were a field of lunatic corn. Dennen called in artillery, and a few seconds later the shells came crashing over. He set the first ones close, no more than fifty meters from their front, and then systematically worked the shells to destroy everything ahead of them. Smoking and pitted, the tracks began moving forward again, keeping close to the lines of exploding shells, only to get hit again. A track went up, and the Old Man pulled them back again, calling in air strikes and leg units.

The gunships flying overhead pulled out, and soon the low-flying phantoms were screaming down the length of the front, dropping napalm. Then the cobras came in again, hovering over the tracks, literally hanging motionless at thirty-degree angles as they popped rockets into the jungle.

Infantry began moving up between the tracks. With the gunships moving out ahead, the column pushed on over ground still smoking from the air strikes and artillery. More tracks were hit, as satchel charges were added to the short, sharp crackings of the M-16's.

Breaking out of the jungle, they hit the base camp. Hundreds of dead gooks were lying on the smoldering, pockmarked mud. They had built a mud rise around the base, and baked by the sun, it was hard as concrete. Two tracks were hit trying to climb over the rise. The rest pulled back and for twenty minutes raked the area with more gunships, H and E, air strikes, and artillery. Then they went in again, and two more tracks were hung up the same way. Again they pulled back and again they threw everything they had at the base. The smell of napalm was so thick in the air that they could hardly breathe. They took it the third time. They were still counting bodies in the morning.

The next day the company was pulled out of the line

and sent back to base camp. During the days they spent resting and rearming, Dennen taught his crews how to skip their bullets into targets. "At 100 or 200 yards you can't tell where your bullets are going. If the ground is flat, you can skip your bullets in. Put them down about ten or fifteen meters in front, and they'll be coming off the ground at waist height. You can use the dirt being kicked up as a guide to where you're aiming."

He tried to figure out ways to save his men. He stacked things in the tracks in such a way that the ammunition was always surrounded by nonexplosives. He even thought of draining some of the gasoline out of the floor tanks, but the Old Man said no.

Three days later, not yet recovered and still short of men, they got pulled out of base camp and sent southwest to fill up the gap left by other mechanized units that had been knocked around themselves.

This time it was the low foothills and rice paddies. Dennen had expected the paddies to be flat, but they weren't. It was the dry season, and they were empty. Their floors were rock-hard, pitted and bumpy. There was no way to move fast or to keep the 50's on target. Hedgegroves ran along the paddies, great tangles of rocks and shrubbery, some big enough to hold whole villages.

As they humped along the uneven floor, Dennen shook his head disgustedly.

"What's wrong, Lieutenant?" his RTO asked.

"Those groves—you could hold one of them with ten men."

The trooper pushed the machine gun out of the way so he had a clear view of the nearest hedgegrove.

Here we go again, Dennen thought. The track tilted almost thirty degrees and then straightened. The dust closed in around them.

"Now they can see us coming. They don't have to wait to hear us."

That night they made a lager in a hedgegrove astride one of the dirt roads that cut through the paddies. There was a village a kilometer away. They took two mortar rounds, and while they couldn't be sure exactly where the rounds came from, they were pretty sure it was near the village, The next morning they swept the area. They took some small arms fire from one of the groves and, wheeling in formation, attacked it. For a few moments the grove was completely hidden by dust thrown up by their rounds. Suddenly the ground shook and a track off to their right rose into the air with a tremendous roar and hung there ten feet off the ground.

"Jesus!" Dennen gasped, watching the twenty-five-ton armored carrier tilt to its side and come crashing down, burying itself in the hard-packed earth. One of the tanks pulled to the left and headed for the stricken track. The whole line stopped.

"What the hell was it?"

"A chicon mine. They put them in the ground on top of fifty-gallon drums of gasoline. They'll turn over a tank, man."

"Yeah," Dennen said. "They really suckered us into that one."

Afterwards they searched the place and found a tunnel that ran the whole length of the grove.

"Hey, Lieutenant, look at this."

Dennen was staring at the track still smoldering in the field. He hated being had. He walked over to the trooper who had called him and was standing by the entrance to another tunnel.

"Look," the trooper said, pointing to some spots of drying blood.

Dennen began taking off his web gear.

"I wouldn't, Lieutenant."

Dennen turned around. It was the Sergeant.

"They spike those damn things," Smith said. "You can put your hand into a scorpion's nest or have a punji stick fall on your head or trip a grenade. Honest, Lieutenant, it ain't worth it."

"If they have time," Dennen said as he finished taking off his gear.

"They don't need time. There are blind alleys in those things already dug."

"Well," Dennen said, "this one I want."

"Here, Lieutenant." His RTO handed him a 45. "It's loaded."

Dennen checked it to make sure. "Sergeant, keep 'em here till I get back."

Taking off his helmet he got down on his hands and knees and crawled into the tunnel. After four or five feet it took a sharp turn to the right. It was stifling, and the dirt clung to his sweat. There was no shoring; the walls were kept up by zig-zagging the hole. With barely enough room to pull himself through, he could hear his breath coming back at him as he pushed himself along, keeping his right hand with the gun out and free in front of him. He must have been crawling for almost ten minutes when suddenly down a long length of the tunnel he saw sunlight ahead. Relieved, he moved toward it when, as suddenly, the light was blotted out. He fired the first round instantly, and followed it with half the clip. A few seconds later the light slowly reappeared.

The Old Man was furious.

"We don't need heroes," he barked. "Dammit, Lieutenant, if you do one more stupid thing, I'll kick your ass from one end of Nam to the other. This is a mechanized unit, understand?"

A week later Dennen was hit. They were sweeping an area north of their base camp and had stopped for lunch. He was squatting on the ground studying his map when an RPG exploded in front of him. His helmet and flack vest took most of the frags; only his legs and arms were hit. They dusted him off to the 27th evac. All he could remember before they knocked him out was the sticky feel when they cut off his pants.

It took four hours in the operating room at the 12th to save his life. We got him in Japan five days later. He was well on his way to healing by then and seemed more concerned about what kind of medical profile we'd give him than his wounds. He did not talk much about the war, though it was obvious from the few things he said that he felt at ease with it and wanted to go back. He liked it —the command, the excitement, the obvious importance of it all. We had to leave in the smaller pieces of shrapnel and hope that eventually they'd make their way to the surface.

"Sure the Negroes don't get promoted as
fast as the whites. You don't see IBM
promoting them either, do you?"

Trooper, 1st Air Cav
Medical Ward
U.S. Army Hospital, Camp Drake, Japan

10

Gentlemen, It Works

Gentlemen, you may smoke. My name is Colonel Griger, Psychiatric Medical Adviser to the United States Army—Vietnam. This hour of your active-duty orientation has been set aside for a discussion of military psychiatry. I know what is on your minds; it is on everyone's mind who is going to war. Let me first try to allay some of your fears. Since you are physicians, it won't be as bad as you think. I've just recently returned from Vietnam and I can assure you that your chances of getting hurt or killed—unless you do something foolish or are somewhere you shouldn't be—are much smaller than right out here on the streets of San Antonio, Texas. I am not saying that Vietnam will not be a difficult place. It is difficult for everyone, whether he admits it or not. The point is to make sure, whether it's yourself or your patients, that when the tour is over those difficulties are left behind where they belong—in Southeast Asia. . . . That is why I am talking to you this hour. To try to make sure that a year's problem does not become a lifelong disability.

"The legs that are lost in Nam are unfortunately lost forever; the eyes that are gone are gone for good. I can assure you, though, that not everyone loses a leg or goes blind. But everyone is afraid and everyone does have his limit of endurance. To fight is to be afraid, and the enormity of that fear can shatter even the strongest man. It will be your job, whether you are a surgeon, internist, or general medical officer, whether you are assigned to a battalion aid station or evacuation hospital, to make sure that the fear is not compounded.

"Gentlemen, there are achievements that come out of any war; most are truly unimportant and hardly worth a

149

campaign, much less a battle. Others are real advancements, a few major human achievements. Believe it or not—and I know it may be hard to believe—one of these major achievements has come out of the chaos of Nam. It is still controversial, but I believe over the years it will prove itself, not only in the military but in civilian psychiatry as well. Those of us in the military have seen it work already. . . ."

"Major Kohler." The corpsman stuck his head into the doorway. "The chopper's in. They got some guy who won't move. Say he's paralyzed."

"OK. Be right there."

The building began shaking again. A moment later another chopper, a Red Cross painted on its nose, inched past the sandbagged window of the office. Kohler watched it from his desk until the whirling blades disappeared from view, then walked quickly out of the room.

Halfway down the hall he heard another chopper passing over the building. They had been coming in like this for almost three days. To keep the beds of the evac hospital open so the new patients could be admitted, everybody who had been admitted before the offensive, even those in for only minor surgery, had been evac'ed to Japan. Whole wards had been cleaned out, and it hadn't taken half a day to fill them up again. The internists were doing all the minor surgery while the surgeons stayed up in the OR on the major cases. The number of psychiatric admissions to Kohler's ward had almost tripled. There just wasn't time any more in the battalion air stations to

150

fiddle around with the combat exhaustions. As soon as they were brought in, they were set aside and sent out on the next chopper. Kohler hadn't slept for almost forty-eight hours.

The corridor was filling up with medics and technicians, and the wounded and dying soldiers were already being wheeled past him to the operating room. They were carrying them in right off the choppers just as they'd been hit, covered with the mud they'd rolled in, shredded apart, pants legs where their legs had been, filthy tourniquets wrapped around the raw, oozing stumps. Some, still in their battle gear, stared up at him wide-eyed, in bewilderment clutching their abdominal packs to their ripped-open stomachs. Others, with vacuum bottles swinging from the bottom of their stretchers, had dirty chest tubes stuck clumsily through their skins. Several, with bandoliers still slung across their chests, were being piled along one side of the blood-spattered corridor—dead.

Kohler reached the admissions and triage area at the end of the hallway. The noise was deafening. The choppers, their rotors still turning, were huddled outside the open doorway, and the medics, bending over to clear the blades, were loading the wounded and hurrying them into the building.

The triage officer with his medics and nurses, all in fatigues and combat boots, met each trooper as he came through the door. They checked his med-evac tags, examined him, and sent him either directly to the operating room, the adjacent emergency area, or the wards. Near the doorway a machine gun stood tilted on its tripod. A chopper, suddenly taking off, went banging through the air over their heads.

"Kohler . . . over there," someone yelled, "near the door."

A grunt, with a bandolier of filthy M-60 ammunition over one shoulder, stood leaning against the wall, cradling an M-16 in his arms.

Kohler was almost up to him before he saw the other soldier huddled on the floor beside the rifleman. He had a med-evac tag tied around his neck, but his fatigues were so dirty and cut up it was impossible to tell his rank or unit. The rifleman came to some semblance of attention, but the trooper on the floor didn't move.

Kohler looked from one to the other. "What's wrong?" he asked the rifleman. "What happened, soldier?"

"Don't know," the grunt said. "He come in just like that."

Kohler had to wait for another chopper to clear the area to make himself heard.

"Who brought him in?"

The rifleman shifted his weapon. "Don't know—wasn't there. We was getting hit, too. Somebody carried him into our perimeter. The medics was just too busy to fuck around with him. The first Dust Off come in, we put him on it."

"He's not from your unit?"

"No, he was with C Company up at Lang Vei. They'd been taking shit for about three days, then yesterday they got overrun. The gooks really whipped their ass."

The grunt made to leave, when he suddenly stopped

152

and turned back to Kohler. For a moment a hint of animation flickered across his face. "They had tanks," he said. "Can you believe it, they took Lang with fucken tanks?" He shook his head and walked out the door to the landing area.

Kohler motioned over a corpsman. "Better take him to the ward. Give him 150 milligrams of thorazine IM and repeat it every hour till he falls asleep, then keep him asleep for at least two days. You can use a wheelchair."

They kept Dienst sleeping for two and a half days, then stopped his thorazine and let him wake up. When Kohler saw him next he was on the neuropsychiatric ward.

There were no locks on the ward, no guards. Despite the diversity of symptoms and patient types, some of whom had been brought in incredibly violent and disoriented, there were no provisions for security. It looked like any other convalescent in-patient ward. All the patients were in T-shirts and fatigues; some were cleaning the room, others sitting alone, reading comic books or writing letters, while here and there were small groups talking among themselves.

Kohler walked through the ward, nodding to those who looked his way. His patients were there to get well, not to dwell on their symptoms. From the moment they were admitted they were expected to get better—or at least to act appropriately. They were still in the Army and despite his own concerns and prejudices, he never allowed them to forget it. Even though the patients were in a neuropsychiatric ward, they still wore their uniforms and maintained their unit affiliations; they were given details, and they obeyed orders. Restraints were necessary occasionally, but only for very short periods of time.

Kohler was surprised at the results. To him, as to so many other analytically oriented psychiatrists off the East Coast, the military machine with its emphasis on interpersonal rather than intrapersonal psychopathology had come as a bit of a shock. At first, he had been frankly skeptical, certain that conversion and anxiety reactions removed without sufficient uncovering techniques would only reestablish themselves in other ways. But his experience with the numbers of patients he had to take care of, no less than the shock of suddenly being dropped into the middle of something as different as war, had quite turned him around.

Before he was drafted he had thought he had it made: a more than comfortable practice, a nice suburban home and family, a good life of reading, teaching, and working. And now, here he was worrying about getting killed, taking care of kids from places he had never heard of, much less even thought about, in a world he had never dreamed could exist, a middle-class psychiatrist treating patients every one of whom had murdered or been almost murdered himself.

When Kohler came to see Dienst, he found the ward master in the nurses' station, charting the new admission.

The ward master quickly stood at attention.

Kohler motioned for him to relax. "Harold, did the neurologist see our boy?"

"Yes, sir."

"What did they say?" Kohler asked, glancing at the chart the ward master handed him.

"Nothing wrong, sir. No neurological reason for his paralysis."

"Good, Harold. And now . . ." Kohler looked out at the ward, "now, for the new psychiatry. You know, sometimes I wish it didn't work so well. I really do."

Dienst was lying on his bed, staring at the ceiling. Washed and dressed in a new set of fatigues, he made no move of recognition as Kohler approached.

"Hi, Corporal. They tell me you can't move your legs."

"Yes . . . yes, sir."

Kohler pulled up a chair. "You've been in Nam how long?"

"Eight months . . . sir."

"In the boonies the whole time?"

"Yes sir—except for a week when I got hit and was at the 45th surg."

"What happened?" Kohler offered Dienst a cigarette.

"No thanks, sir." Dienst seemed to relax a bit. "We got ambushed. I took a piece of a claymore in my hand, sir."

"What happened this time?"

Dienst looked blank.

"What happened, that you got evac'ed this time?"

"I don't really know, sir.

"Well, what is the last thing you remember?"

Dienst thought for a moment. "The tanks, I guess," he said hesitantly.

Kohler waited. "Then?" he prodded. Dienst suddenly looked very nervous. "Then?"

"I couldn't move."

"This ever happen before?"

"Huh . . . ?"

"Your not being able to move—did it ever happen before, at home or at school?"

"No. No, sir."

"Were you scared?"

Dienst looked confused.

"It's OK," Kohler said, waving away his question.

"Yes, sir."

"We're going to talk about this a few more times. Everyone handles fear and difficult situations—like you were in—in their own way. For some, it's diarrhea; others can't see, some can't move. This paralysis you are experiencing now will pass. We'll talk about it, though, so you'll be able to understand exactly what happened to you. Why you became paralyzed, and why you're here. But while we're talking, I expect you to go about your normal duties and to listen to the ward master and corpsman.

"But I . . ."

Kohler held up his hand. "That means everything," he said matter-of-factly, though pleasantly. "The mess hall is down the hallway about twenty meters. That's where the patients in this ward eat. We don't serve food in bed here."

Dienst looked terrified; adolescent confusion and fear was etched across his lean sunburned face. "But . . . but I can't move," he said desperately. "I can't move my legs."

"Yes, you can," Kohler said softly, "but if you don't want to, you can crawl there." he stood up. "Or go hungry. It

156

doesn't matter to us. Whichever way you want it will be fine. I'll see you tomorrow."

The next day the ward master called to report that Dienst hadn't moved.

"No lunch?" Kohler asked.

"No sir, and no breakfast either."

"OK, Harold; I'll be right down to see him."

"Sir, the 45th surg just called in. They got three guys there, looney as hell, but they can't get 'em out till maybe tomorrow. They're really gettin' hit hard. Two Dust Offs got lit up trying to get into the LZ; their surgeon's dead. The medic running the show wants to know what medication to zap these guys with."

"Tell him to give 'em 250 mgm of thorazine IM each, every four hours till they're asleep. Tell him not to worry, just get 'em to sleep."

"Sir, would it be OK with you to go out with the Dust Offs to get 'em?"

"What if you get lit up?" Kohler said. "You know how important you are to the ward, Harold. The blacks need you there. They need to see a black face in charge."

"It's my old unit, sir. I could help them."

Kohler hesitated. "OK, then, but watch yourself."

Dienst didn't acknowledge Kohler's greeting. His eyes were sharp and focused, but he still lay staring into space.

Kohler sat down on the edge of the bed so that Dienst had to shift his weight. The movement broke the rigidity of his posture.

"You look angry," Kohler said. "You're still in the Army, son; I expect you to look at me while I'm talking to you."

Dienst reluctantly turned his head.

"You must be hungry," Kohler continued matter-of-factly. "You know, I've looked through your 201 file, and you've been a fine soldier. A bit stubborn, maybe. You must have been strong-willed all your life. That's an important thing to be. Not many people are."

Dienst frowned. He looked confused.

"I know you're hungry. You haven't eaten here, and I know you didn't have time to eat where you came from. Where was it again, now?"

"Lang Vei."

"I bet you didn't do much complaining there, either. I mean, you're not a complainer."

"No, sir," Dienst said, softening.

"Tell me what happened out there," Kohler said softly. "Tell me, son. Tell me about the tanks."

"Gentlemen, what I want to do now is give you a history of military psychiatry, the theoretical basis for our recent advancement, and why we in the military feel that it works.

"Freud is dead. He was a great man, but we simply can't use him any more. Let me read to you two quotes from one of his disciples, from a book published in 1957 called Captain Newman, M.D. *Captain Newman, an Army psychiatrist during World War II, is the chief of a psychiatric service at a large Army hospital. I quote:*

> *We deal with sickness, the kind of sickness that doesn't show up on sphygomographs or fluoroscopes. A patient may run no fever, or hit 104 out of the blue. Don't think they all babble gibberish; most of them make sense, if you listen to*

their vocabulary long enough and hard enough. They're using English, but speaking a foreign language—the language of suffering, which requires special symbols. A man can have a pulse that suddenly beats like a trip hammer or one that doesn't register much more than a corpse's. There's a reason, there's always a reason. To call someone mad is meaningless. There is only one thing you can be absolutely sure of; every, I repeat, every man who's on my ward—no matter what he says or what you hear or what the textbooks say—is sick.

"Now if that's not enough, there's this—I quote from another chapter:

> "What's worrying you, Newman?" asked his ward master.
> "Jackson's hallucinating again. He dived under the bed before breakfast, yelling the Japs are here and he wouldn't come out. He keeps screaming and shivering and begging to go home."
> "Did he get his medication last night?"
> "Yes, but it's worn off."
> "Have you tried to coax him out?"
> "Nurse Blodgett spent half the morning on the floor."
> "A man would be a fool to come out for old frozen puss. Has he eaten anything?"
> "No."
> "Does he have any special favorites in food?"
> "Chocolate malts."
> Captain Newman wrinkled his brow. "OK. You put a nice big chocolate malt and some cookies on the floor, right near the bed. Let him see you. Tell him he'll hurt my feelings if he isn't back in his bed when I start morning rounds."

"None of it sounds quite right, does it? A little too occupied with illness and a bit too sentimental. But during the Second World War it was the Newmans expressing just those concerns who were running all the military *psychiatric services. The Newmans were not so much wrong as ill-equipped to handle the war; they tried, but in most cases just compounded the difficulties; and the V.A. hospitals, twenty-five years after the war has ended, are still catering to their patients. Chocolate malts are a good idea, but there were too many patients and not enough malts to go around. The Newmans got lost in the flood of military patients and ended up in their concern and confusion by declaring a frightening number of healthy men incapable of military service, to be discharged to the V.A. hospitals nearest their homes.*

"A few facts: During the early years of the Second World War one out of every four soldiers evacuated out of the combat area was evacuated out as a neuropsychiatric patient, and one-half of the medical discharges granted at the time were granted for psychiatric disability. It was not a new problem. The Freudian-oriented Newmans were just handling it in a different way. Combat neurosis, battle fatigue, exhaustion, whatever you want to call it, has always been a problem of battle. In the First World War it was called 'shell shock.' The psychiatrists, unfortunately, had a part of that too. If you came out of the battle or bombardment unwounded but sweating and shaking, disoriented, paralyzed, or simply unable to go on, you were diagnosed as having been too close to an exploding shell. The psychiatrists, trained and experienced in the organically oriented institutionalized psychiatry of the late nineteenth and early twentieth century had decided, presumably because they had to say something, that these visibly shaken men had something truly wrong with their brains—not their minds, but

their brains. They concluded that the concussion from the exploding shells must have in some strange way rattled these poor soldiers' brains. Despite hundreds of fortuitous autopsies that showed no evidence at all of brain damage, they persisted in giving these boys a diagnosis of shell shock and with it the implication of irreversible destruction of brain tissue.

"It was a convenient theory. If the shell-shocked patient recovered completely, the concussion had not been severe. If he did not, the damage was complete and irreversible. If the patient intermittently lapsed back into bizarre behavior, the damage lay somewhere between the two extremes. The disaster, though, of all of this squeezing of observable facts into an established though inappropriate theory, was not that these men were labeled, but that the label, once attached, was encouraged and the diagnosis maintained not only by the psychiatrists but the patient himself, his family, his friends, and a nation that demanded each one of its boys be a hero. The shock wave from the exploding shell was a convenient excuse for everyone, though in truth a deadly one. The shell did it all. The patient was just too close to the explosion. To admit otherwise would have meant that the patient, the son, the father, the lover, had indeed failed, that he had been a coward, that he had been unable to take it and run away, leaving his buddies out there to die. It was as difficult to admit then, as it is now. . . ."

"Look Dienst," Kohler said, "I know things were tough and you'd been pushing a long time. Believe me, there is an end point to anyone's resources. There's a place when all the will power, motivation, training, concern, and leadership simply isn't enough any more. Everyone handles that point in his own way. Some guys decide to surrender, or say fuck it and charge. Some panic and get killed; some even decide to just sit there and get court-martialed. You're too tough for that, though, and too concerned. You might be a bit too brave for all of this. No, no, I mean it. But let's talk more about you and how you do things later. Still, I have to repeat, we don't serve in bed here. I want you to get to the mess hall on your own. I know, I know," Kohler said, raising his hand to keep Dienst from complaining, "but this isn't a hotel. When you go back to your unit . . . you're going to have to walk."

A sudden terrified look swept over Dienst's face.

"You'll be able to go back," Kohler said. "I know it, and so do you."

"Gentlemen, once the symptoms were admitted and the guilt placed elsewhere, these symptoms persisted, maintained by an ever-deepening inability of the men to admit their failure, a failure that grew deeper and more pernicious as the distance from the battlefield grew and the original terror was forgotten. Right or wrong, warfare is a very manly thing; to fail at it, even in its most subtle forms, is to challenge one's whole masculinity. Failure is difficult for an adult to handle, and for an adolescent, impossible. Unfortunately this is not just rhetoric; even today, fifty years later, there are still old men who, because of a few hours or days of cumulative fear and ex-

haustion and a misdiagnosis, have been consigned by their doctors, families, and even themselves to hobble uselessly about hospital floors.

"The psychiatry of the First World War missed a very important point—the fixation of symptoms. These troopers were ill—but it was their guilt and unconscious feelings of failure that fixed their symptoms and turned what should have been circumscribed reactions into lifelong debilitating conditions. A few psychiatrists, though, some of the front-line French and German physicians, saw what was happening to these men once they were removed from the fighting and published papers showing that the evacuation of shell-shocked cases to rear areas only produced chronic disability."

That evening Kohler was working in his office when a 122-mm rocket hit in the middle of the grounds. It landed fifty meters from the operating room, blowing in the door and killing a corpsman and a nurse. Everyone waited for a second one. All through the rest of the compound, doctors, medics, and patients stopped, waiting for the next rocket. Kohler, sitting alone in his office, waited like everyone else, chewing nervously on the end of his pencil. Nothing came. Either there had only been one or the others hadn't gone off. Sighing, he went back to work and a few minutes later the phone rang.

"Good. Just let him crawl there. I know, he's trying to embarrass us. Yeah, he's just showing the world how little we understand and how brutal we are. Just let him crawl. He's testing us and himself. The important thing is that he's moving. I don't care what the nursing supervisor thinks," Kohler said angrily. "He has to crawl before he can walk. I'll see him in the morning. Oh, and listen; get him some new fatigues when he gets back. I want him to know we know what he's doing."

"Between World War I and World War II an attitude developed among the Freudians that analysis would be to mental illness what penicillin had been to infectious diseases. In their enthusiasm to heal the world they forgot that at best the world is a difficult place. Just delve long enough and deep enough, sweep away the defenses, uncover the conflicts, bring them to light, resolve them in an adult way, and the suffering will disappear. They presented the people with a Freudian right not to suffer. In its own way this idea was as blinding to the psychiatrists of the Second World War when it broke out as the organic theories had been to the psychiatrists of the First.

"In 1941 there were fewer than twenty fully trained psychiatrists in the whole Army. During the early days of mobilization, these men, like so many other career officers, were transferred to command and administrative positions, leaving the responsibility of the every-day practice of military to the newly inducted psychiatrists. The war struck, and the Newmans—right out of their analytic training—fell headlong into it.

"There was no more nonsense about shock waves and concussions. When you went under in 1941 to 1945 it was not because of shock waves rattling your brains, but the sudden surfacing of emotionally unresolved, though per-

sistent conflicts. *The soldier who broke did not break so much from the fear of having someone trying to kill him or even from the harrowingness of battle, but from some neurotic tendency, deep-seated, that had always been there eating him away, or ready to eat him away.*

"The Newmans had been trained to address themselves to the eradication of psychiatric symptomatology, to intrinsic psychopathology, to the symptoms of conflict within the patient. Armed with what were essentially individual theories and techniques, they were suddenly presented not with one or two patients, who, subjected to the normal stresses of living, had decompensated, but thousands who had been exposed to the unique and terrifying prospect of war. Viewed from the outside, the Newmans' reactions to this flood of patients was either to withdraw into the spotty use of intensive psychotherapy or simply to wring their hands and abandon the mass of patients to the V.A. system as treatable only if more psychiatrists were provided, which of course they weren't."

"Major Kohler."

"Yeah?" Kohler said, looking up at the corpsman without bothering to take his feet off the nearby chair. The doctors across the table stopped talking.

"Another chopper's in. The ward just called. Seems like you got a real winner."

Kohler put his glass down on the edge of the table. "What's wrong?"

"Black power. Apparently he took on half his base

camp. They sent him here with four citations, under armed guard—and in a straitjacket."

"Did Harold see him?"

"Yes, sir. He's the one who told me to find you."

"Is the kid lucid?"

"Yeah, I guess."

"OK. Tell Harold to take off the cuffs and jacket. Well, go tell him," Kohler said, sitting up. "I'll be right there."

"What about these fellows?" one of the doctors asked.

"Huh?"

"What about these Negro troopers?"

"What do you mean, what about them?"

"Are they . . . ? I mean, do they carry their own weight?"

"How long have you been here?" Kohler asked dryly.

"Two months."

"Why don't you wait about six more. Nothing like long-term reality to rid us of our foolish little prejudices."

Without waiting for an answer Kohler got up from his chair and left the room.

The ward was quiet. "Where is he?" Kohler asked the ward master.

"In the treatment room, sir," Harold said. "He didn't want to move, so we left him there."

"OK. What do you know about him?"

"Name's Leroy Washington. Medic—25th Division . . ."

"And," Kohler interrupted, "got taken away from his unit and rotated back to a base camp, was there for about ten days, and just got freaky as hell."

"Well, a bit more, sir. He took on a lieutenant and broke a captain's jaw and then went after a couple of hundred MP's."

166

"Drugs?" Kohler asked.

The ward master shrugged.

"And what about Dienst?"

"He's getting tired of crawling."

"I'll see him this afternoon. I'd better see Washington now."

Kohler went to the treatment area and, pulling aside the curtain, walked inside. The trooper, a short, stocky Negro, his right eye battered shut, was sitting sullenly on a cabinet. The straitjacket was lying on the floor. Kohler gave him a quick, appraising look.

"We won't need that anymore," he said. "Nobody makes it through six months as a field medic and then goes goofy unless somebody pushes him, does he?"

"Gentlemen, not only were the Newmans sending these combat neurosis patients home, but they were also losing these same men to their units and ultimately to the war. The Army simply could not tolerate the losses. They wanted these men back to duty."

"The ward master tells me this morning he gave you an order and you essentially told him to go fuck himself."

Washington remained seated, expressionless.

"I'm white," Kohler said, "but let me tell you what I think's bothering you. It's not that captain you cut down or the ward master or even me. It's that you go through all that shit, risking your life for white or black, for God and country, and then they take you out of it and it's the same shit that you left. If it was me, I'd be angry too, angry as hell. Angry at the United States, angry at my officers, but most of all angry with myself for being so fucken stupid as to think anything would change. Believing that if I did my job it wouldn't be the same. Yes, angry at myself for believing all that bullshit about comradeship and equality, angry with myself that, despite all my willingness, not only to join in but to put my life on the line, it's still the same fucken mess it always was. I'd be furious, man, furious."

Washington was stunned, and Kohler could see that he was stoically fighting not to let any part of him show. He watched the clear, smooth adolescent face twist on itself, saw the sadness and the depression underneath.

Come on, he thought, come on. Let it out. Let it out.

"The idea that the interpersonal aspects of adaptation had to be considered as well as the intrapsychic began to catch hold, and be pushed by Army psychiatrists. Then, more and more civilian psychiatrists began to think that it might be inappropriate to think of personality development solely in terms of resolved intrapsychic conflicts. The thought developed that no matter how mentally ill a patient might seem to be or indeed was, there were still areas of his ego that had been left intact, and that if one dwelt on the ill fraction, the conflict-ridden part of the ego, supporting only that part of the personality to the exclusion of the rest, you might very well be fooling yourself as to how sick the person really was and, quite simply, merely be prolonging the whole affair. With a little ex-

*perimentation, a few military psychiatrists who, in des-
peration, had operationally taken up these new ideas,
began to get remarkable results. In its simplest form,
their success had to do with expectation."*

"You look a bit sad," the ward master said.

"Well, maybe I am," Kohler said. "Tell me, Harold, why
the hell do the blacks come into the Army anyway . . . ?"

"They get drafted."

"I know. But why do they show up for induction?"

"It's their country."

"You want to tell Washington that?" Kohler said.

"I mean, they think it's their country. You know, most
of these kids are middle-class. No, I mean it. They're not
extremists. They're told to do something, and they do it,
just like anybody else. But," Harold said quickly, "there
is something else. You've never been in a ghetto, have you,
Major?"

"No, I haven't."

"Well, it's not very good living, and it's not just the
way Middle America thinks of it. I had an apartment once,
on Indiana Avenue in Chicago. It had holes and rats all
the time and hot water every now and then. I worked like
hell to fix it up—painted the walls, covered the holes.
And when it was all done, the landlord jacked up the rent.
I couldn't pay it, and since it was the nicest apartment on
the block, he had no trouble finding a tenant who'd pay
the higher rent. So, how do you cope with a situation like
that? The Army comes along and, despite their misgiv-
ings, the ghetto kids go. At least they get three meals a

day and have a little money to spend. For some, Doctor, it is the first time in their life they have enough without having to do something wrong or going hungry. Besides, their brothers are here. Compared to what they're used to, the Army ain't that bad."

Kohler got up to leave. "I'm learning, but I'll tell you this. The only way the Army is going to learn is when the squads start coming back from patrol all white or all black."

"Label a soldier as mentally ill, support that illness, show him that it is what interests you about him, and he will be ill and stay ill. Expectation, gentlemen, expectation."

"Anger, Leroy," Kohler said, "anger's a funny thing. It can be a way of hiding things from ourselves. Tell me a little about your growing up, what you remember about it—about being black."

Washington shook his head, as if to say what's the use.

"You know, Leroy, the black psychiatrists who deal with black children report that a child experiences his first prejudice as early as two years. How old are you?"

"Eighteen."

Washington talked slowly at first, but later more and more animatedly—swinging into his words and concerns, not complaining so much as just talking about being a black child in a white world.

"And then you went into the medics," Kohler said, "and you weren't black any more. You were a healer, a savior, a medic—you could put everything aside for a while. And then it was over and you were back to being black again."

"Yeah," Washington said grimly, "I sure was."

"You see, Leroy, there's another side to your anger. It hurts a man to be called a nigger."

"The idea spread that perhaps the important thing about a soldier who cracked was not his illness, but his health. That perhaps when a trooper did come apart—no matter how bizarre the disruption—there was still a central pillar of personality left intact and functioning, a central core that could be dealt with at the same time that the illness was being treated. Prodded by the military, the psychiatrists began to use some of these "perhaps" operationally, and they found that central core and began to understand the astounding effects that guilt had on the fixation of symptoms. It became obvious that the evacuation of combat neurosis from the front was not a cure—but part of the disease; that it was best to treat these boys as far forward as possible; that their unit identification should be maintained and, above all else, the treatment should always include the unwavering expectation, no matter how appearingly disabling the symptoms, that these boys would be returned to duty as soon as possible."

The phone rang.

"Major, there's a Mr. Tamni here from the Criminal Investigation Division."

"What does he want?"

"He's here about your patient, Leroy Washington."

"OK. Send him in. You'd better go," he said to Harold. "Criminal investigation, for Christ's sake."

A moment after the ward master had left the office there was a knock at the door and a brisk, pleasant-looking man in civilian clothes walked in. "Hello, Major. My name's Tamni. I'm assigned to the 529th Military Intelligence Detachment."

Kohler motioned him to a chair.

"It's about your patient, specialist fifth-class Washington. He's under investigation for assault and battery." Kohler waited for him to go on. "We'd like to know your feelings about his mental status."

"I see," Kohler said. "His mental status. If the Provost Marshall wants a psychiatric evaluation of this patient, he can request it in writing."

"We know that, sir. But we were hoping for a bit more. This man was . . . well, he was one of the troublemakers in his brigade."

"In what way?"

"There were racial overtones to what he did."

"So?"

"You know, the Army is concerned with this kind of dissent. We'd like a fairly definitive evaluation."

"Mr. Tamni, I would advise you to do your investigative work yourself. That is what I believe you are trained for. I will do what I am trained for, no more. Now, if you will excuse me, I'm a very busy person and I assume you are."

Tamni got slowly to his feet.

"I will tell you this, though," Kohler said. "He's sane,

eminently sane. But the Army made a bad mistake with him. They made him a medic, gave him respect and an important job, and then rotated him back to a base camp where he was harassed, abused, given menial jobs, treated like a stupid nigger, and told to mind his own business. I'm certifying him fit for duty and recommending that he be sent back to his unit. And I'll tell you something else. You'd better learn how to investigate guys like him and learn how to do it well, because you are going to be spending a lot of your time on soldiers just like him."

"Gentlemen, the Korean war began in the middle of all these new concerns. For the psychiatrists, it began much the same as World War II ended. There is, unfortunately, a certain inertia to military thinking that at times, I admit, can be numbing. The lessons of 1943 and 1944 were simply forgotten and the psychiatric cases were once again being treated the same as all other medical cases, as sick people who should be removed from the combat zone. Six months into the war, the number of psychiatric patients being evacuated from the front were up to early World War II levels. The shocked response of the military was quicker, though, this time, and the new theories and methods that were already on the shelves were quickly put into use. To repeat, they entailed: (1) treatment of patients as far forward as possible to eliminate the fixation of symptoms; (2) maintenance of unit identification to contain the anxiety of being suddenly alone, from adding to the already developed anxieties; and (3) the unwavering ex-

173

*pectation that these patients, no matter how bizarre their
symptoms, would be returned to duty as soon as possible."*

"Excuse me, sir," the ward master said, "is something
wrong?"

"I don't know."

"Like Washington?"

"Yeah."

"What are you going to do with him?"

Kohler sighed. "Try to get him back to duty. What I'd
really like to do is make him white."

"Or make everyone else black," the ward master said.

Kohler had to smile at the thought. "What I'm trying
to do is make him look at the reality of what he did and
what he is. What's bothering him is that he lost control.
It's the whole identity crisis all over again. What am I?
Who am I? I have to be his sounding board, sort of give
him permission to be angry with the whole damn mess
and appease the guilt that goes along with losing control.
Try to get him proud of being black. Now, how the hell
can I do all that?"

*"Why, then, gentlemen, does a soldier crack? If it's
not from the shock waves or a blossoming neurosis, what's
left? Well, quite simply, war itself and exhaustion. Let
me read from the reprint you were handed when you
walked in":*

> *In combating fear, the combat soldier employs a good deal
> of his energy. There is an end point in the available resources*

174

of any individual. There is a place in time when all the positive motivation, training, and leadership are not enough, when the soldier's capability and willingness to continue begin to deteriorate. If there is no chance of relief or no additional factors to sustain him, the potentiality for combat exhaustion exists. It is also important to note that this energy juncture may begin to indicate his impairment as a soldier in spite of his physical presence. His judgment is not as good, alertness may suffer, and his willingness to take chances may disappear. He and his men may become physical casualties long before they become psychological casualties.

This exhaustion is also partly physical. No rule exists as to which—mental or physical—exhaustion is either more prevalent or important; they both play important roles. Physical exhaustion is more comprehensible than the other factors mentioned. Nearly everyone has, at one time or another, expended about as much physical energy as possible in a certain period of time—whether during a football game or a strenuous evening of activity—the feeling can readily be recalled by anyone. In many ways, the symptoms of exhaustion are similar to those resulting from fear. In combat, they are mutually reinforcing.

"Sir, Dienst is here to see you."

"OK." Kohler rose from behind his desk.

Dienst entered the office. He looked a bit embarrassed.

"I just wanted to thank you, sir."

"Come in," Kohler said. "Sit down. Take a load off your feet."

"I don't have much time," Dienst said. He was dressed in his jungle fatigues with his bush hat perched on the top of his head. "I'm going out this morning. All I wanted to do was say thanks."

"No," Kohler said, "you've got it wrong. It is I who should be thanking you. You'll do fine. Write me and let me know what's happening."

"I will. I mean, I promise."

"Good luck."

"Well, Major, I made it through nine months; I can make it through three more."

"No need for psychiatric contortions; no shock waves; no need to conjure up deep-seated anxieties and conflicts. It is combat exhaustion—instead of something ominous and mysterious. It is, quite simply, just having had too much. Of course, in more technical terms, combat exhaustion can be thought of as an abnormal reaction to the stress of combat, its manifestation being unique to the person who develops it, channeled into a specific form by the person's own individual personality and background experience. But it is only one of many abnormal reactions. A soldier who has had too much might choose to surrender or convulsively go forward. He might panic and get killed; he could get himself wounded or wound himself; he might even go to the chaplain or decide on the relative safety of a stockade. He might—if he's so disposed—develop psychosomatic complaints, get angry, or, in some cases, become totally unreasonable. He can become neurotic, begin to shake, refuse to move, or go completely hysterical. He might even become grossly psychotic—hold imaginary rifles, hear voices, or see his grandmother in every chopper that flies by.

"You will be treating these men, and the treatment is

simple. For most it will just be rest. In more severe cases, those soldiers whose functioning is beginning to be impaired, who can't rest, you will medically put to sleep. They are given enough thorazine to put them out and left alone for a day or two. They too, though, like the troopers who are merely resting, stay near the aid station. The more disturbed patients, those troopers who for the moment may be truly disoriented, who have completely stopped functioning, who for any number of reasons appear to need more than a short rest, are sent to an evacuation hospital. But they are never lost to their units. Their group identity is never tampered with, and they know they will be going back. And they do go back. And they are accepted by their units. Believe me, the casual, yet efficient way it is all handled, the official emphasis on health rather than disease, and the lack of mumbo-jumbo have taken the stigma out of having had too much. To the men, it is just something that happens; and more important, it is something they realize can happen to anyone. It is handled that way and it is presented that way.

"Gentlemen, it works."

It works, thought Kohler, but the war goes on. The new psychiatry has done nothing about that. There were 11,000 wounded last month; two fire bases were overrun, and 700 boys were killed. We used to believe that conversion and anxiety reactions removed without sufficient uncovering techniques would only go on to re-establish themselves in other ways. No more of that now. In Nam the psychiatric patients go back to duty. One hundred percent of the combat exhaustion, 90 percent of the character-behavior disorders, 98 percent of the alcoholic and drug problems, 56 percent of the psychosis, 85 percent of the psychoneurosis, 90 percent of the acute situation reaction—they all go back with an operation diagnosis on their record of acute situation reaction. No ominous-sounding names to disturb the patients or their units.

It works. The men are not lost to the fight, and the terrifying stupidity of war is not allowed to go on crippling forever. At least, that's the official belief. But there is no medical or psychiatric follow-up on the boys after they've returned to duty. No one knows if they are the ones who die in the very next fire fight, who miss the wire stretched out across the tract, or gun down unarmed civilians. Apparently, the Army doesn't seem to want to find out.

"After six months they promoted our colonel and sent him to Washington. It's not that he's a liar or a bad guy. It's just that he likes this shit. If they listen to him, they're fucken crazy."

Trooper, 101st Airborne
Orthopedic Ward
U.S. Army Hospital, Camp Drake, Japan

11

Bosum

THE officers who run this war survived World War II. They remember, as if it were yesterday, what it was to lose a division in an afternoon and then go on to worry about losing an army. They remember what it was not to be ready and then not to have enough. It was their youth, and even today, thirty years later, it is what happened then that forms the comfortable base on which they work and argue. They are not dishonest officers, nor are they particularly shortsighted or brutal; if anything, they are incredibly sincere and dedicated men who unfortunately are locked into the early 1940's. For all their professional and at times personal restraint, though, they desperately want to win, or at least not to lose, and are always, even within the shifting quagmire of Nam, pushing a bit, trying for a better way.

Bosum had been trying for quite some time. It was not his first war. He'd been in Burma and Korea. Things had been tougher then, much tougher, but they had never been so confused or muddled. In Nam, he'd been assigned to MACV as an operations adviser to the ARVN's and spent his first five months in country trying to understand what was expected not only of the South Vietnamese Army but the Americans as well, and what could be done to satisfy those expectations.

It had been a tortuous pursuit, during which, despite himself, he gradually became uneasy about the whole thing, then plainly doubtful. No one seemed to know anything. When he questioned his superiors about how many men they thought they'd need to do the job, nobody seemed to know; worse, no one knew exactly what the job was. When he asked if the bombings of the north had been effective, the field Commander said no, while the Air Force officers said yes. When he asked if the recent troop buildup had changed the complexion of the war, the answer was no. When he asked the ARVN Commanders about deployments and orders of battle, they just shrugged. He came to realize that despite what was said, the only real United States policy was to send in more and more troops to fight more and more communists. The number of villages pacified, the amount of area held and people won over were simply manufactured data distributed, as necessary, withdrawn, and manufactured again.

The only realities he found were the soldiers and the gunships. The weapons and troops he agreed with; what he opposed was the sloppy, inconsistent way in which they were used. There was no commitment; everything was done in dribbles. And with the dribbling went a constant, never-ending shifting of resources and concerns. No one knew what was going on. The only thing everyone agreed on was that they were killing people, but the killing, Bosum realized, wasn't enough. With it had to go the understanding that the killing and terror must go on until the whole thing was over. If Vietnam could not be handled politically, then at least the solution should be found on the battlefield.

The tail, it seemed to Bosum, could wag the dog, but during his time with MACV he kept his thoughts to himself, supervised what he was supposed to supervise, and continued to write his trim, efficient reports.

From MACV he went to Headquarters, USARV. He began by inspecting the field units, going on patrol with them. He found the troops universally sloppy. They smoked on patrol, played radios, and dropped cigarette butts and candy wrappers around ambush sites. Some even lit fires at night. They fought well when they fought, but they seemed to give no thought to the fighting until the shooting began.

If there was any morale at all, outside of the mutual concern of a fire fight, it was a morale of time. He had never seen troops so fatalistic. Even at the worst in Burma, when the only thing between the Japanese and India were 15,000 poorly equipped United States and British troops, there was nothing close to the soporific fatalism he found gripping the GI's in Vietnam. The troops knew that if they made it 365 days without getting killed or wounded they were done. It would be over without even having to look back. Everything was geared to that departure date —their hopes, their concerns, their plans. Friends, if there were any, came next, and then maybe the VC. It was an impossible way to fight. He could only wonder how the troops did as well as they did.

Bosum was up with the 1st Air Cav when they tried to take hills 837 and 838. Two companies tried for three days, and finally, after almost 80-percent casualties, they drove the VC off the hills. He stood there in the valley and watched the helicopters come to take the troopers home. Perhaps he was too old-fashioned not to feel a bit foolish to have seen troops fight so hard to get somewhere only to be taken home just when they got there. But this wasn't to be a war for land.

He went back to headquarters in Saigon and wrote a factual report on what he had found. All the units were understrength; platoons that uniformly were to hold forty-seven men ran with thirty; ambushes were poorly arranged and carried out; LRRP units were not being used effectively; booby traps were not standardized throughout the same unit; body counts were not reliable. The report was fully documented and endorsed. Again he kept his more subjective thoughts to himself.

After almost eleven months in Nam, he was transferred from Headquarters, USARV to the 25th division as a brigade commander, fighting in the Central Highlands. The unit he commanded had been fighting and tracking for almost three weeks. Four times in those three weeks their LRRP units had made contact with at least a regiment of the 17th NVA division, only to lose them again before any significant battle could be pushed. They kept finding bits and pieces, vicious little fire fights here and there, but nothing big, nothing that would really hurt anybody. Not that the men cared. Like so many other units, they fought well enough when they had to, but in between they gave little thought to the fighting itself.

Bosum watched it all for one week, then ordered that the LRRP units, after making contact, were not to withdraw but were to stay where they were and harass the enemy. They were to set up ambushes and keep after Charlie until the units they fixed were hit.

It was not a very popular order. The six-man LRRP teams were Ranger units, scouts, and trackers, who were always traveling in unfamiliar terrain and were always outmanned. They never knew the best places for an ambush, nor, for that matter, the best escape routes. Once they committed themselves, they were always running the risk of being cut off and hit themselves. In the first two weeks after his order, three teams were caught and wiped out. He added more men to each unit, giving them more fire power and turning them into heavily armed recon patrols. In the next week two more got hit. He finally put together three LRRP units, and they worked for two and a half weeks—ate up parts of two North Vietnamese companies, fixed a regiment for the brigade, and got out. The mission was an unqualified if unpopular success. The recombined unit had taken 60-percent casualties.

The lifers accepted it all. Their colonel wouldn't stay there forever, and there was some logic behind what he was doing. Besides, the units were hardening up.

To give the Brigade more hitting power, Bosum rearranged the weapons platoons, putting two men to a machine gun instead of three. He took the third man from each platoon and created another machine-gun group, giving each platoon 50 percent more support fire. It was a lot more to carry, tough, and with only two men to an M-60 instead of three, there was no reserve if either the gunner or feeder got hit, and no cover. The troopers didn't like it, and when a platoon on ambush got overrun, the word spread that the machine gunners got it first and left the unit without heavy weapons support. By the end of the week the men were blaming the Colonel for the disaster. They had stopped thinking about home.

The ambush procedures were changed. Instead of one platoon taking part, three were assigned. When a good track was found, the center platoon became the killer group, setting out claymores in series of four and taking up positions directly behind the mines. The other two platoons filled out along the track. Bosum's orders were that no one was to open fire unless the odds were no more than two to one, or the group to be ambushed could be contained within the flanking platoons. There was less rest for everyone, but the brigade started getting 80-percent kills. They began to hurt Charlie.

With the increase in sweeps and ambushes, their own casualties began going up. Units that had been running at three-quarters strength began drifting down to under 60 percent. Eight- and ten-man squads began humping it, still carrying, under Bosum's orders, the fire power for the regular twelve-man patrols. Nothing was left behind. They were getting just as tired as they were getting tough. Still, the number of casual mistakes and booby-trap injuries began going down. Men quit smoking grass on patrol and began leaving things behind that might jingle.

Division Intelligence reported that the North Vietnamese were beginning to be leery of the brigade's area. There were even some reports that the 17th was pulling out. Bosum decided to really push them. Without clearing it with headquarters, he told his commanders that from now on, after making contact with the enemy, they were not to have their units pull back in order to call in artillery or gunships; instead, they were to keep pushing in with all they had. He was sure the techniques of making contact, pulling back, and calling in support strikes gave the enemy forces a chance either to regroup or to filter out of the area. It also tended to keep his men battle-shy.

The company commanders went back to their units and spread the word. Troopers who before had been rather oblivious to it all and had spent their free time feeding the ants or smoking grass began wondering when the next fire fight would be. For the first time, they began sharpening their knives. Trackers and tiger scouts didn't bother to write home before going out.

Three days after Bosum issued the orders, a patrol was ambushed, and the relieving patrol got pinned down. He committed another company, then two. The fighting spread. Air strikes hovered overhead, but the fighting was too close to get in. Bosum threw in another company, then the reserve. There was no time to get the wounded out; Dust Offs were cancelled and told to stand by. Over a thousand men were fighting, most within three or four meters of each other, in jungle so thick you couldn't even see who was firing at you. It went on for hours. Bosum asked Division for reinforcements, and they airlifted in another company. The men kept fighting, pushing, and when it got dark, the units were so tangled up with each other they couldn't disengage, and the killing went on through the night.

Whole platoons were wiped out. Squads of North Vietnamese were killed where they lay. By two in the morning the fighting turned into hundreds of terrifying individual battles. Boys killed one another in the dark, shredded apart by automatic fire from no more than a meter away. The wounded, lying broken on the ground, whispered hoarsely to passing figures, only to be killed. At first light, the Vietnamese began pulling out. The orders were for prisoners, but the bitter and exhausted survivors shot them down where they found them.

It had been an expensive victory. Division was a bit concerned about the casualties, but they decided to wait

187

to see what effect these new tactics had on the enemy before they passed judgment. As for himself, Bosum was impressed. For the first time, the area was clear of NVA, not because the communists had decided to move, but because they had to.

The next night, after he had gone to sleep, somebody rolled a grenade into his tent. Bosum died on the ground, waiting for the Dust Off.

"What the fuck, they're trying to kill me and I'm trying to kill them. Who gives a shit."

Trooper, 4th Division
Psychiatric Ward
U.S. Army Hospital, Zama, Japan

12

Me Either

I'M gonna kill the fucker . . . no, don't say a word; he's dead and that's it."

"They'll just send another one."

"I don't care about the next one, man. This is the fucker that's got to go."

"Listen Cab, it could be trouble."

"Where the fuck do you think this is—paradise? Look around you. You blind or something? What the hell else can they do to us?"

"How you gonna do it?" one of the troopers asked, shading his eyes from the sun so he could look at Cab.

"Shoot the fucker down, man; just shoot 'em down."

"It ain't gonna be easy," Tracy said.

"Look," Cab said, slinging his M-16. "The RTO calls him down and when he comes down, we light him up. It's that simple. Bamb! Another chopper gone, man, that's all it is."

"What happens when they find him shot to shit with M-16 and M-60 rounds?" Trowl asked from the back of the group.

"I've got two AK's broken down at the fire base. Next sweep we'll just take them along."

There was a long, heavy silence, broken only by the sporadic crack of a distant sniper round. "What about the First Sergeant?" Trummer asked.

"He's out here, man; he ain't anywhere else. You don't see him sitting in Saigon, getting fat. Don't worry; when that chopper goes down, he ain't gonna be running over to see who's left to save."

"OK," Kolwitz said, getting up from where he was squatting. "We kill him, but only this one. That's it—no more!"

"What about the chopper pilot?" someone asked from the back of the group.

"He's got to go, too."

"Do you know who he is?" the trooper asked. "One of the guys back at the TOC told me MacGreever's flying the Old Man now. He ain't got long till his DEROS."

"That's tough, man, but you can't shoot down half a chopper."

"I ain't for killing MacGreever," Trowl said.

"Me either," Johnson said, slamming his weapon closed. "He brought us in those 50's that night, man, and he didn't have to do it."

"Count me out," Trowl said defensively. "I ain't killing MacGreever just to grease some fucking Lieutenant Colonel."

"Me neither," Tracy said, taking off his helmet and licking the salt off his lips.

"He flew Dust Offs, too," someone else offered.

"Count me out," another trooper said, nervously fingering the safety on his weapon.

"Me too."

"Me either."

"The gooks use greenish-blue tracers.
I swear to God they're lovely coming
up at you."

Chopper pilot
Surgical Ward
U.S. Army Hospital, Zama, Japan

13

Choppers

BY the time you read this, over 4000 helicopters will have been shot down, a third of all the chopper pilots who have ever been to Nam will have been killed or medically boarded out of the Army, and the average life span of any loach pilot, whether in Nam, Laos, or Cambodia, will probably be down to somewhere around three months. But they still volunteer. There is not a Volkswagen in a parking lot at Fort Rucker, Alabama, or at Hunter in Georgia, nor a Scouter or Ford Fairlane running their roads. It's all Honda 500's and BSA Scramblers, Corvettes with the heads lowered, and Dodges with 3-11 rear ends. The kids who choose to go there are of a type—lean and tough, mechanically oriented, obsessed with speed and daring, and incredibly brave.

My God! One moment the chopper was there, charging in protectively across the perimeter, tail up, and the next it was gone, torn apart in a monstrous ball of flame. For a moment, the sheer unexpected violence of it all held them. Stunned, the troopers looking up from the mud, watched what was left of the chopper come hurtling headless out of the flames, a great torn piece of steel plunging blindly on across the paddy.

Southeast Asia has become, above all else, a helicopter war. The slow, bitter attrition of Dien Bien Phu, the gradual strangulation of a whole army simply cannot happen now. We might lose a platoon or a company, maybe even a battalion—but never an army. You can't mass against gunships or charge through miniguns. And it is difficult to demoralize troopers who know they are half an hour from the nearest hospital or ten minutes away from a cold beer or a hot meal.

Like the troopers themselves, the Pentagon has come to realize it's a helicopter war. After years of proudly pointing to the skies we own when it is the land we are fighting, they've come around. The Huey Tug, a product-improved Huey that will have the power to hover out of the ground effect as high as 4000 feet and at 95 degrees with a 6000-pound payload, is currently being developed under military contract by Bell Helicopter Company. The Kowa OH-58, a light observation chopper, will continue to be bought by the government with $64.2 million provided by the military through 1971. The Chinook Ch-47 medium transport helicopter will be funded at the $41.6 million level. The development of a heavy-lift helicopter with a payload of twenty to thirty tons will continue with a $21 billion budget. Another $17.6 million will keep the Cheyenne AH-56A armed assault helicopter under development.

They are not very pretty. Even the tiny, glass-domed loaches—that can hover motionless fifteen feet off the ground and pour machine-gun fire through the six-inch slit of a pill box, or slowly and maliciously track a man down a narrow jungle path—look out of place in the air. Helicopters have none of the grace of an airplane and even less of the style. They have to tug themselves off the ground—and once in the air they stay there, churning on through the sheer power of their engines. If anything happens to that power—and it doesn't take much . . .

Choppers

A single AK round is effective up to 1200 feet; a Russian-made 51-caliber machine gun can get up to 5000. A part of a 37-mm anti-aircraft shell is good almost anywhere. In Vietnam, though, most choppers are destroyed in the thirty feet between landing and taking off. At Rucker and Hunter they call it the area of translational flight, that time between hover and forward flight when the lift from the rotors is decaying and the lift from the forward flight has yet to build up. The stresses on the gear train and the rotor system are fantastic. If anything happens then, if the rotor goes or a round grinds up the gear box, if the hub freezes, or the hydraulics foul, there is no time to change the pitch of the blades and not enough height to allow for auto rotation. It is straight down. The gooks could, if they chose, put a few rounds into a chopper at 800 feet or even 1000, but that might give the pilot enough height to get it down. So they wait until the chopper is too low to glide and too low to hover, and then they light it up.

"6/36, 6/36 . . ."

"36/6," the radio crackled over the clearing.

"6/36, we have thirteen WIA, six KIA, have managed to regroup and set up an NPD with Bravo Company."

It was almost dark. You could just begin to see the reddish glow of the tracer rounds heading out into the tree lines.

"36/6 sortie."

"6/36." The Sergeant stopped for a moment to keep the blood from running into his mouth. "We've burned out thirteen tubes and we're scraping the bottom of our ammunition."

A greenish-blue tracer round arched overhead, hit the top of the track, and whistled off up into the air. The Sergeant and RTO pressed in closer against the warm steel of the APC.

"36/6," the radio crackled again loudly, cutting off for a moment the rattle of small arms fire, "we have Charlie model gunship. It can deliver sortie. Stay on this push."

An M-60 opened up on their right. It was soon joined by the sharp whipping sound of 50's.

"36/6 . . . 33 Sierra is near Quin Yon. Dust Off notified."

Ten minutes later the Dust Offs were over them. The firing picked up. Reddish tracers were skipping out from every quadrant of the perimeter.

"They're gonna rush us," the RTO said. "Sooner or later, they're gonna really hit us."

The radio interrupted. "36/ Dust Off 3. Request smoke."

The Sergeant motioned to the RTO, who wiped the sweat from his hands and picked a smoke grenade out of his webbing.

"Dust Off 3/36 roger that," he said, shifting his position a bit to let the radioman slip by. An RPG whistled across the NPD, exploding with a blinding flash near the flame track.

"36/6 Dust Off 3, is the LZ secure?" The Sergeant waited while the RTO, head down, zigzagged toward the darkening perimeter.

"Dust Off 3, negative. Repeat, negative."

"36, can you give effective suppressive fire?"

Another RPG hit in front of the hedgegrove just as the

RTO was throwing the smoke. Blown back, he lay there twisting on the ground, while the thick green smoke curled back over him.

"Negative. Dust Off 3. Repeat, negative."

There was a long, crackling pause. Over it, they could hear the choppers.

"36, Dust Off 3. Got green smoke."

"Dust Off 3, confirmed—green smoke," the Sergeant said, turning to face the choppers.

They were coming in low and quick—two of them, switching from side to side to shake off the gooks' aim. The first Dust Off came in right over the trees and went straight into the ground at over eighty knots. The second suddenly cut out, drifted out over the perimeter, and then, with its engines howling, quickly cut back toward the landing zone. Above the ground fighting, they could hear sledge-hammer blows as the 51's slammed through its thin, aluminum skin. The Huey sputtered a moment over them and then skidded heavily into the LZ, cracking its landing gear. It sat tilted on its broken skid while the pilot, his adolescent face drawn tight and thin, leaned out the window and motioned for them to hurry. He kept his rotors turning while the medics, moving swiftly through the great clouds of swirling, choking dust, carried on the wounded and dying. When it was loaded, he got it light on its broken skid, lifted it a few feet off the ground, then quickly spun it around. Giving it full power, he got it moving along the ground. At about fifteen feet it started taking fire—a dark shape moving out across an even darker sky. The troopers on the ground could see the bright greenish-blue tracers bracket it, then lose them-

selves as if the chopper were some kind of color damp-
ener. It kept moving along at the same height until finally
—out of sight—its engines sputtered and the craft, rising
suddenly out of the jungle, drifted off to the left and was
gone.

A second later, the darkness behind the NVA positions
was broken by a brilliant flash of yellow-green light. Fifteen minutes later the gunship arrived from Qui Nhou.
Over the rockets and mortars and the intermittent rattling
of automatic fire, they could hear the dull thudding of
its turbine engine churning toward them through the
evening sky. The NVA heard it too and stopped firing.
Listening, they raised the sights on their weapons and
waited.

It had taken over a hundred and fifty years, a century
and a half of trial and error, sometimes without theory,
always on faith, to go straight up. It took more than just
providing a curved surface and a power source to move
that surface through the air, to develop a helicopter. It
took a whole evolution—a desperate and at times deadly
struggle between man with his dreams, and physics with
its laws.

For over a hundred years, since the middle 1880's, foolishly shaped machines had kept trying to fly by going
straight up. In almost every country, from Holland to
Italy, wood-framed monstrosities were built, tested,
crashed, and rebuilt again. A few did manage to get into
the air, some even stumbling forward a few yards, but
none really flew. Not only were the early helicopters

under-powered, but once off the ground, they tended to spin embarrassingly about their centers, and if flown forward too quickly would simply flip over. The maneuverability was atrocious, and directional control was almost impossible, but the helicopterists continued. Without knowing what was wrong men tinkered with their mistakes until they found the answers, persisting despite the laughter and the danger until one by one each problem was solved by solutions so definitive and so structurally necessary that even today every chopper that rises in Nam carries in its modern configuration the whole history of its race.

The early spinning was found to be the result of torque —the tendency of the engine to twirl the chopper one way while it rotated the blades the other. This was solved in the early 1920's by extending the tail of the craft and mounting, not an engine, but a small rotor on the end of the extension—that little propeller you see spinning at the back of every chopper today. The propeller works off a drive shaft coming off the main rotor engine. When the engine speeds up to give the main rotor more rpm's, the anti-torque propeller speeds up as well, literally pushing the tail back in place, offsetting the torque the engine is developing to spin the craft. But the forces are still there, and when they are let loose today they are as disastrous now as they were funny back in the 1920's. It doesn't take much: if the shaft from the main engine goes or the blades themselves are hit, if the tail is damaged or the tiny rotor is shot away, the physics of the whole affair takes over and the chopper begins to swing to the left. The fuselage begins to turn on itself. The gathering centrifugal forces push the pilot and co-pilot against their armor-plated seats, the crew chief and door gunner against their aluminum-sheeted walls. All control is lost, and like some crazy spinning top, the chopper, gathering momentum, begins whipping around itself, whopping through the air, spinning faster and faster—all the way down. It is a new way of dying—unique and very modern.

The flipping over, even at minimal forward speeds, was finally solved, without anyone knowing why, by the fortuitous assembling of flexible blades for the main rotors. It was only much later that the reason for these blades' success was discovered. The problem was asymmetry of lift. The ability of the rotating blades to overturn the craft was found to be due to the unequal lifting power of the advancing and retreating of blades—the advancing blade picking up speed and therefore lift with the forward movement of the helicopter, and the retreating blade losing speed and relative lift as it swung back around the hub away from the forward direction of the craft.

At forward speeds of as little as twenty miles an hour, this dissymmetry between the advancing and retreating blades provided an unequal force great enough to overturn the early choppers. The flexible blades—flapping up and down under the increasing and decreasing lift— allowed the rotor system and the blades themselves to handle the unequal forces without transmitting them to the aircraft frame itself. Later, with more powerful engines and the need for stronger nonflexible blades, the new blades were flexibly hinged to the rotor hubs, giving the drooping effect so familiar today.

But the solution was at a price—an articulating rotor

hub is an incredibly complex piece of machinery. The intricate hinges and flaps that allow the eight-foot, 1000-pound blades to rise and fall while they're spinning at 1800 revolutions per minute are difficult to maintain and service. Linkages can rapidly weaken, rotors can freeze; the numerous hinges and flaps necessary to allow the blades to twist and turn continually fatigue and wear out. At best, under the most ideal conditions of support and supervision, things go wrong. In Nam, where chances must be taken and where there really are not enough choppers to go around, the helicopters are overflown and under-maintained. At eighty knots and a thousand feet it is the same as dying.

By the late 1930's the helicopter, at least in its present configuration, was basically finished. It took a few more years for the problems of directional control, maneuverability, center of lift, and ground resonance to be solved. Linkages that worked directly through the rotor hubs were added. The cyclic and pitch control were improved. Gears were perfected, and engine power was increased. By the time the chopper was ready, though, the world had become beguiled by the grace and speed of the Spitfires and numbed by the destructive power of the Stuka and Liberator. The choppers of the early 1940's were still a bit too clumsy for all that flash. They vibrated, and fully loaded, they had a poor center-of-gravity travel. There were still understandable concerns about rotor bearings, blade strength, and frequency of repair.

You'd think that the military would have pushed for an aircraft that could land anywhere, hover for hours about an area, and supply close-in continual aerial support. But the fighters and bombers were rolling out of the factories, and the military could afford to be skeptical. Even today, thirty years later, it is still the few Migs shot down, the Phantoms, and the carrier-based Skyhawks that hold the glamour.

"I guess I could have said no, but you sort of don't think about it; I mean, you don't say it, anyway. I guess you could call it a frame of mind. You know, there are guys out there that need you. I mean, you see how they live—sweeps during the day, ambushes at night, the shitty water, and the heat—dirty and wet all the time. It's not just for a while, it's for months. Some of them are out there for a whole year. I mean, they're just like you, same age, same feelings, only they're stuck there on the ground, and at least we can get clean sheets at night and a beer. Nobody talks about it, but you can see it on their faces everytime you come into an LZ. They know you'll be there; the Dust Offs have to go in whether the landing zone is secure or not. They try at least once. Hell, I knew a Dust-Off pilot who went into a landing zone that was being overrun. The rest of us—the guns and the guys that fly slicks—if it's hot, we can just as well hang it up. But that don't make it any easier for the guys on the ground. They're still there. It's hard to forget.

"Like I said, I could have refused the mission, but the 25th had been fighting all day, they'd burned out all their 50's, and had gone into a night lager while the gooks were still pushing 'em. Two Dust Offs had been lit up just a few minutes before, but they needed the barrels. The gooks were really getting their asses up to hit 'em during the night or early in the morning. There should have been a Chinoock around, but it was getting dark fast, and it was too far away to sortie. I was the only one close enough to get to Quin Yon and back before the place really got shocked in. So I said yeah. I knew the LZ would have to be hot.

"Anyways, I had that gunship so fucken loaded with water cans, boxes of 50-cal ammunition, barrels, and medical supplies I couldn't even get it off the runway at Quin Yon. I was bringing them everything I thought they could use, see. Hell, the damn chopper was so heavy I had to bounce it down the runway to get enough air speed to lift off. I swear to God I had the skids smoking before I got it up.

"By the time I was over the LZ, it was pretty dark. I asked them to mark it, but I couldn't see the smoke. They used a strobe, but I couldn't tell how big the zone was. Their sergeant taking me in told me about some trees. I asked for strobes around the zone, but they didn't have enough. I had to turn on my landing lights for a second, then come around again. Maybe I shouldn't have used the lights, but I had to. I mean, it just gave the gooks a better chance to line up on me. That second time I could hear the 51's over my own engine, but I was too busy trying to get us down. I just told the door gunner to open up, and I kept her going in. I got to the bottom of my approach when I started losing engine and rotor rpm—I was just too damn overloaded—Christ, the g's on the hub must have been tremendous. I pulled back on the pitch to get some more pressure on the blades and I just made it.

Man, did I come in steep. Just cleared the trees, and bamb!—right in. It was like a controlled crash landing. I bounced the portside skid off the top of the track. I took the wounded out with me and I swear to God I clipped the same damn trees going out. I went around three times like that, Quin Yon and back. The third time they got us, killed my door gunner and co-pilot. But dammit, they sure as hell had enough practice."

"It's not your country. How long will you
be willing to stay there?"

Japanese nurse
Pediatrics Clinic
U.S. Army Hospital, Zama, Japan

14

Joan

I'M telling you," Justice said, waiting impatiently while Kelly, in the next bed, struggled to get the straw into his mouth. "I'm going back to the 4th Division and I don't know any more now than when I got here. This time they'll fucken kill me."

Kelly sucked noisily on the straw. Unable to turn his head, he was forced to look at Justice out of the corner of his eye.

"I'm not kidding, man; we couldn't keep a point. The first time we went out we got lost. Circled the base camp for three hours. Hell, even when we do move it's like a herd of fucken elephants. Everybody smoking grass, things jingling all over making noise. I know guys been high since they got to Nam. They're paranoid as hell."

"I know, I know," Justice went on defensively. "I'm as bad as everyone else. We ain't the 1st Air Cav, I'll be the first to admit, but that doesn't make it right."

Talking to Kelly, he didn't see the nurse until she was there standing between the beds.

"Sorry," she said pleasantly. "Mind if I borrow your friend for a minute?"

Kelly pulled the straw out from between his teeth.

"Mind helping?" she asked Justice.

"No, not at all," he said, swinging his feet over the edge of his bed.

The nurse took Kelly's glass of juice. "This isn't going to hurt," she said, putting the glass down on the night stand. Brushing the hair out of her eyes, she bent over the bed and began unrolling the length of gauze from around the soldier's chest.

"Here." She handed the gauze to Justice. Despite her

sweat-soaked fatigues, there was a faint odor of perfume about her.

She turned back to Kelly. "This won't hurt," she repeated, lifting the edge of the chest pack.

"What part of the States you from, ma'am?" Justice asked, looking over her shoulder to watch what she was doing.

"Kansas," she said, carefully peeling the packs off Kelly's wound.

"Jesus!" Justice exclaimed, staring open-mouthed at the wound. It ran in a great jagged line from Kelly's wired jaw, down across the front of his neck, through his shoulder and out again across the upper part of his chest, reaching down his front to the bottom of his ribs. Great wads of muscle had simply been ripped away; his collar bone was gone, and at places down the front of his chest the wound was so deep you could see the lung, shiny and pink, moving in and out against the inside of the ribs.

The nurse took some sterile scissors and began cleaning the dead skin from around the edges. Kelly sat rigid, staring straight ahead of him.

"I figured you were from the Midwest," Justice said. "I've been through Kansas once with my family; pretty flat. Live there all your life?"

"Most of it."

"We'll leave off the gauze," she said to Kelly as she put on clean packs, "until the doctors come by. Do you want anything?"

Kelly shook his head.

"Your wounds are coming along fine." Turning to Justice she took back the soiled bandage.

"Been here long?" he asked.

"About a year."

"Phew, that's a long time."

"It gets long," she said.

Justice couldn't keep his eyes off her. She was a big girl with a good figure, and she had a pleasant midwestern face, open and plain, but pretty, and it would be pretty for a long time. "If you won't mind my saying so, Miss . . . Lieutenant," he said stiffly, "I've never seen anybody looked so good in fatigues before."

"I look better in a dress."

"You look fine right now."

"Thanks," she said good-naturedly. "Now your turn."

"Me?" he looked surprised. "I'm OK."

"You got in this afternoon, didn't you?" she asked, looking at her chart as she motioned him to take off his pajama top.

"Honest," he said, "it ain't much."

"Well, let's see it anyway."

He had trouble getting his shoulder free.

"Here," she said, helping him. "Turn a bit more."

Twisting around on the edge of the bed, he let her see his back. A thick, puckered surgical scar, held together by heavy black sutures ran across his upper back.

"Can you move your arm?"

"Pretty much," he said, lifting it up and down.

"Now across."

"Wooo . . ." He grimaced. "Can't do that too well."

"It's OK," she said, helping him back with his top. "The doctors will be around to see you later tonight. They're still up in the OR."

"How long before you think," he said, trying to be nonchalant. "I mean, before you think I'll be going back?"

"To your unit? You've got a good three weeks. How much longer do you have in country?"

"Nine months."

Her smile faded. "What do you do?" she asked.

"Eleven Bravo."

"It's a tough job," she said softly. "But you know, after about six months they'll probably pull you back from the front. What unit are you with?"

"Fourth Division." Justice pointed to the unit patch pasted over his bed.

"Are you married?"

"No, but I hope . . . I mean, I expect to be."

"What's her name?"

"Rebecca." Embarrassed, he glanced over at Kelly.

"Any pictures?"

"Lost 'em when I got hit. They sort of got blown all over."

A chopper coming into the hospital flew directly over the ward, shaking the building, and they had to stop talking until it had passed.

"How did it happen?"

"Well . . . I was just sort of sitting around, doing nothing. Our platoon had made a sweep and we were waiting for the choppers. There were four of us, two 11 Bravos, and two engineers, and we decided to go get some water. I walked out on the track. Christ, I was even dragging my rifle in my left hand. I hadn't gone five meters when— crack! It was like getting clobbered on the shoulder by a baseball bat. I started to fall when I realized it wasn't too good a place to crash, so I just dropped my rifle and started running. They fired a burst, but it went behind me into the trees. I guess. They figured they'd had me, and when I started running, it sort of took them by surprise. They must have been setting us up for a good fifteen minutes. The only thing that saved us was my walking out by myself. If it had been all of us, they would have lit us up with everything they had."

"You made it, though," she said supportingly. "It will be over soon."

"Yeah, one way or the other."

"Twenty thousand go home a month."

"I know," he said absently. He was looking at the name tag sewn on her fatigues, too shy to let his eyes rest on the curve of her breast.

"It's officially Lieutenant Allen," she said, "but here it's just Joan."

"I like Joan," he said, trying to sound matter-of-fact.

She went on to the other patients. Everyone who wanted a sleeping pill got one. Sometimes she gave two and three; 400 or 500 mg of seconal was not uncommon, and no one ever checked the sleeping-pill inventory. It's hard to rest, much less sleep after you've spent a few months crawling through the jungle, and these boys came in right out of it. No transition; one moment a healthy eighteen- or nineteen-year-old out there, and the next he's torn apart, lying in a hospital. Every noise gets to them; just the corpsman walking by to take a temp or blood pressure sets them off. Half a year or half a week of looking for the flash off a rifle barrel or freezing at the crack of a twig—nobody can really sleep after that, nobody, so they have to be drugged. It might not be good medicine, but it keeps the wards quiet and lets the corpsmen do their work without having half the patients jump up every time they hear his steps. It helps, too, if the hospital should get hit during the night.

In the eleven months that Joan had been working at the 312th, her hospital had been mortared five times. It was in a valley, which made it easier to hit. Two of the attacks had been just a round or two; the other three had brought out the gunships. One time they almost got through the wire, and the alert had gone red.

She had wakened the patients then, putting them sleepily on the floor below the sandbag line. The corpsmen helped her, while the ward master opened the ward supply and got out the M-16's.

The patients in traction were left where they were and covered with mattresses from empty beds. And all the while the cobras and gunships came roaring in, crisscrossing above them, their turbines whistling in a kind of high-pitched frenzy. The noise shook the building, and they had to scream at each other to be heard. She had put herself on the floor between two of the critical patients. A rocket had gone off outside the building, the noise crashing over the ward like a concussion. With a blinding flash, another rocket went off, this time closer.

"Don't worry, ma'am," one of the patients said, looking down over the edge of his bed. "I've been through this lots of times. It ain't bad."

Not bad, Joan thought afterwards. But the medical

ward was hit, and the ward master, one of the doctors, and six patients were killed.

It had only happened like that once, but the attack did break up the routine of lots of work followed by lots of boredom. During the malaria season, the 312th averaged forty to fifty medical admissions a day—sick kids collapsing on their way through the door. Malaria for some units is a 72-hour disease. You have to have a fever of 102 or above for three days before the battalion surgeons are allowed to make the diagnosis of malaria. And all that time you are still out there in that 110-degree heat.

"Why don't they take their anti-malaria pills?" she'd asked.

The ward master smiled. "If they knew they'd be evacuated as soon as they got sick, nobody would take 'em. The 72-hour thing is a way to keep them straight."

The number of surgical admissions, though, depended on the level of the fighting. During a big push they ran seventy to eighty major cases a day. At first the vocabulary as well as the wounds had shocked her. "Ten hummers today and six rotacery cases—Christ!" the ward master said, looking at the admissions list. "Rotacery cases—do their abdomens and then you have to turn them over and do their backs."

She assisted in cases where the surgeon, opening the shattered abdomens of boys still in their teens and faced with a belly full of blood, had to decide within seconds whether first to take out the battered and bleeding spleen, go after the lacerated liver, and clamp the torn vena cava, or start with the hole in the renal artery.

During the offensive through the Ashau, she had not

slept for almost a week. When things slowed, though, and stayed slow, it was worse.

There was nothing to do except endure the heat and discomfort. There was no privacy and never any place to go. The fellows, even the doctors, were transient, and outside the perimeter nothing was secure. In the eleven months that Joan was in the country she had left the 312th only three times, each time against orders.

The first time was four months after she'd arrived. It had been a brutal three weeks before that; she just had to get away. She had gathered her courage and, ignoring the order that no woman was to leave the base, asked one of the docs to drive her out the gate to the dispensary at the 2nd Field Force. The 2nd Field ran their Med Caps from the dispensary. Smiling innocently, fiddling with the top button on her blouse, she lied again, telling the Med Cap officer about having permission, and got on a Med Cap chopper going north to the ARVN compound at Dalat. The morning Joan hitched a ride, the compound was hit. There was some thought at the dispensary about canceling the mission, but there were too many wounded, so they went anyway. It was a lovely trip. Joan sat in the doorway of the chopper with her feet dangling over the edge and watched the rich browns and greens of Nam pass under her. The sky was a deep crystal blue.

A cobra—tough and lean—kept pace the whole way, while a loach darted nimbly along in front of them. A few miles from the LZ the cobra suddenly pulled up while the loach, dropping, moved on ahead. The crew chief, putting his head close to her ear, yelled above the noise of the engine that the village was still taking fire. At the

LZ the loach circled protectively overhead, while the cobra stayed up and circled counterclockwise above the village. The pilot brought them in, but didn't land—instead, he hovered the craft three or four feet off the ground. An armed escort surrounding the LZ motioned frantically for them to hurry. Jumping off with the rest of them, she ran hunched over with the others toward the compound. The escort moved along with them, and in the background she could hear the sharp, high-pitched cracking of machine-gun fire. The cobra, churning down, roared in over them, the racket of its miniguns shattering the air. Startled, she had tripped and stumbled headlong into the dust. Scrambling to her feet, she kept running. At the dispensary, she pushed away their hands. "Welcome to my last Med Cap," she said indignantly, pushing the dusty hair out of her eyes.

The wounded were laid out on the ground behind the dispensary. There were five of them; the dead had already been carried away.

Like all Vietnamese they were incredibly small, almost delicate. Their families, expressionless, squatted around them, waiting. They set up in the dispensary, nothing more than a hut that had been set aside for medical work, and began taking care of the patients. Everything was done under local anesthesia, the wounds cleaned and packed, the cuts and lacerations sutured.

After the wounded were taken care of, they opened the dispensary to general sick call—first the paratrooper advisers, then the ARVN troops, and finally the villagers. The advisers had a medic with them. He handled almost everything; there was not much left to be done. The

ARVN's, though, were a different story: boils, abscesses, rotten teeth, thirty new VD cases, diarrhea, vomiting—they all came walking through the hut, everyone smiling, and Joan, wiping the sweat out of her eyes, began to feel ill from the heat.

Finally, when the ARVN's were through, they moved outside the hut to see the villagers. No matter what was asked, they nodded: "Yes. Head hurts." "Yes, chest, yes, stomach hurt?" "Yes, legs," "Yes." The Docs shrugged it off and, ignoring the rampant tuberculosis and tumors, just passed out aspirin and iron pills. Joan gave the bicillin shots—two to four million units for any infection—and handed out the diarrhea mix for any kind of diarrhea. It went on for hours.

Just as they were ready to leave, a woman came into the compound carrying a limp child whose leg, abscessed from the knee to the thigh, was twice the size of the other. Two of the little girl's toes were already turning black from the pressure. They put her on a table and while they held her down, the surgeon took a scalpel and made an incision down the length of the abscess. Without a sound the child closed her eyes and fainted. The corpsman collected the pus in an empty fruit tin. He filled it three times before the oozing stopped. They put in a drain and made arrangements for her to be evacuated to the 312th the next morning.

"Is it always like this?" Joan asked, sponging off the table.

"No," Major Norris said, cleaning his equipment. "Sometimes we get a few VC. Why so surprised? These people have been fighting now for thirty or forty years.

It's a way of life; they've come to grips with it as best they can. The VC leave their guns at the gate, and we take care of them."

"But . . ."

"No buts. Look," he said quietly, "there is an informal structure around here. It's quite different from what we say, Saigon says, or even the VC say. It may seem foolish, but not to these villagers. It's like reaching an agreement with your infection. I won't hurt you if you don't hurt me. We'll just exist together. It's like this," he said, putting away the scalpel into his medical kit; "we're in the ARVN compound, the village is around us, and around the village are the VC. If they wanted, they could take it; it would cost 'em, but they could take it. So everyone lives together." He looked at her and shrugged. "I know, but it's not my war. In five months I'll be home, and this will all be like it never happened."

Joan went on two more med caps; there was nothing noble in her going. It takes an idiot to think you can win a war or even help a country with bottles of aspirin and cough medicine. She went just to get away from the 312th. Just to do something different.

After six months in country she had her R and R in Hong Kong. She met a naval aviator on leave from Thailand. He might have been married, or he might not have been; she never asked, and it bothered her not a bit that she didn't. Before she left for Nam, she sent home over six hundred dollars worth of dresses, perfumes, and wigs.

The hardest thing to get used to when she got back was the heat. She'd forgotten. The rats and bugs didn't bother her, but the heat. . . . She was just getting used to it once more when the bombing halt began and the Kellys and Justices started coming in again.

Joan had finished her evening rounds about 8:30 and sat down at the nurses' station to do her paper work. The nurses' station was in the center of the ward, and from her desk she could see down all four radiating wings. After she'd been at her work for about ten minutes the phone rang. It was the nursing supervisor telling her they were getting in two more chopper loads that night.

It had been like that for days. Whereas before the halt, the VC and NVA seemed to be picking their targets, saving their stuff like RPG's for squads and platoons, now they were using it on individual troopers. She must have heard the same story Justice had told her ten or twelve times since she'd gotten back.

The two Dust Offs came in half an hour later. The 45th surg was being hit again, so the Dust Offs had to overfly it and go the fifteen minutes farther on to the 312th. Two frag wounds, a head injury, and a cord transection came into her ward. Two abdominal wounds and three traumatic amputations went right up to the OR. Two troopers died on the chopper during the extra fifteen minutes it took to get to the 312th.

It was almost midnight when she was able to sit down at her desk again. Except for the small lamp coming down over the top of her desk, the ward was completely dark. Sighing, she took out her flashlight and laid it on the desk beside the lamp and began again on the charts. She had been working for some time when Justice shuffled up to her desk in his slippers.

"Hi," she said, laying down her pen. Cigarette?" She pushed her pack across the desk.

"Thanks," he said, sinking into a chair. "Go on with your work. I'm having a little trouble sleeping."

"I don't want to sound nursy," Joan said, "but would you like another sleeping pill?"

"No, thanks," Justice settled himself more comfortably into his chair. "They make me groggy."

"How about some milk, then? It's fresh."

He struck a match to his cigarette. In the harsh light of the flame, she was shocked to see how much older he looked than he had before. She got up and walked into the kitchen directly behind the nurses' station. Justice followed her with his eyes.

"Do you like it here?" he asked when she handed him the cool carton of milk.

"No, I want to go home just like everyone else."

"How old are you?" he asked suddenly.

"Thirty-five. No," she said, laughing at the look on his face. "I was only kidding. I'm twenty-two. My God, do I look thirty-five?"

"No, ma'am," he said quickly. "It's just that you sort of surprised me." Lowering his eyes, embarrassed, he busied himself with the milk.

"Well, don't let it bother you," she said. "No make-up, fatigues, combat boots, and pigtails can surprise anybody. Tell me, what are you going to do when you get out?"

He thought for a moment as he ground out his cigarette in the ashtray. "School, I guess."

"Where?"

"University of Idaho, probably. I don't want to get too far from home, not for a while, anyway. I did pretty well in high school. Some things I did pretty well in . . . like history," he said proudly. "Guess I won't have any trouble getting in. I mean, being from the state and everything; besides, I'll have the GI Bill."

He was reaching for another cigarette when they both heard it—a dull, ominous thud—far away, but carrying heavily through the night air. The match suspended in his hand, he stared blankly at Joan. Then the windows along the whole north side of the ward lit up, and a tremendous explosion crashed in over the building.

"Get under the desk," Joan said, switching off the desk lamp. "Under the desk!" Even as Justice was moving, a second explosion seared over them, followed by the confused rattling of automatic fire. She was switching on the flashlight as the first corpsman came running into the ward. The sky lit up again, and there was another explosion, close enough this time to rattle the desk. Other corpsmen came running in.

Some IV bottles crashed. In the shadowy light the corpsmen were hustling patients onto the floor. Five more explosions went off; the last one shattered the door and blew it in across the room. The corpsmen threw themselves down with the patients.

"Sappers!" someone yelled. The phone rang and went dead.

"The guns, dammit! Where are the guns!" All over the ward, patients were running for cover. A burst of automatic fire cut through the wall above the bag line.

Joan stumbled through the dark, toward the traction patients. A mortar round, exploding with terrifying noise, took away the north end of one of the wings, sending fragments down the rest of the ward. People were screaming; fires seemed to be burning everywhere. She tripped, and was getting to her feet when a second round went off.

The blast came in through the window and, searing past her, lifted her up and threw her against one of the striker frames. The ward was a shambles. Bodies were sprawled all over the floor. Bed frames, twisted and broken, lay in the smoke and dirt. Corpsmen, coughing, on their bellies, were passing out M-16's, sliding them along the floor, while right outside the wing a series of smaller, less powerful explosions were going off.

"Grenades . . . get your head up . . . shoot, dammit! Those are grenades, dammit, those aren't satchel charges. They're through the wire. Idiots . . . shoot! Grenades . . . grenades!" The sergeant in traction was still yelling commands when the first AK rounds cracked through the ward, killing the ward master and a patient near him. A moment later a grenade came through one of the windows, bounced once on the floor, and exploded. A second burst enfilated down the center aisle. Shadows moving against the flames ran back and forth outside the ward. Over the explosions was the sudden high-pitched cracking of M-16's and M-60's.

In the confusion and smoke the surviving corpsmen were sliding ammunition along the floor to the patients near windows and doors. A corpsman had just slammed a clip into his M-16 when a figure passed in front of the hole that had been blasted through the wall; he emptied the clip into the figure. In the dust and smoke, hardly able to breathe, two corpsmen, along with a patient, were crawling up to one of the walls when an exploding RPG blew it in and killed them. Stunned by the explosions, those who had weapons rolled over on the floor and began firing into the dust where the wall had been. Two figures came tumbling through the smoke, their AK's bouncing along the concrete floor.

Suddenly the whole night was lit up by the blinding metallic flash of a star shell. It flooded in through what was left of the place. Then the gunships came in. They swung in above the ward, hovering protectively over its smoking ruins, firing in one long continuous roar.

A few minutes later, the camp's reactionary force managed to secure the ward and the perimeter. When they found Joan, she was lying where she'd been thrown, crying, her left leg folded grotesquely under her.

"A lot of people are getting fat out of this, the correspondents, the engineers, the so-called consultants. They don't have to be there, Man, they ask for it, and I hope to fuck every one of 'em dies."

Trooper, 9th Division
Intensive Care Unit
U.S. Army Hospital, Zama, Japan

15

$90,000,000
a Day

L ET me tell you about that defoliation program. It don't work. No, I mean it. It ain't done a damn thing it was supposed to do. I'll give 'em there are a lot of dead people out there because of it, but not theirs—ours. The whole idea was to prevent ambushes, to clear the area. Some idiot somewhere sold somebody the idea that if the gooks couldn't hide, then they couldn't ambush you, and they bought the idea, I mean really bought it. The trouble with the whole thing is that the VC and NVA use guns in their ambushes instead of bows and arrows. Nobody mentioned that. They don't have to be sitting on top of you to pull off an ambush. An AK-47 round is effective up to 1500 meters and accurate up to 600. So we'll hit an area, like along a busy road, billions of gallons of the stuff, and pretty soon there's nothing except some dead bushes for fifty or even 300 meters on both sides of where the road or track used to be. So the gooks will start shooting at you from 300 meters away instead of five, only now you're the one that ain't got no place to hide. Ever try running 100 meters or 200? It takes time, and they're firing at you the whole way. And I mean the whole way."

Thirty billion dollars a year, three million dollars an hour, and God only knows how much for a project that doesn't work. Chemicals from Ohio, factories in Georgia, hundreds of trucks, a freighter a month, steel cylinders, diluents, cargo helicopters, squadrons of specially equipped duster aircraft, guages and valves, contracts and subcontracts—it's part of the other Nam, the ninety-million-dollar-a-day Nam.

❁ ❁ ❁ ❁ ❁

"I'm sorry."

"Look, it's on your way—two, three minutes."

"I'm sorry," the pilot said indifferently.

Herman shifted the box to make it easier to carry. "There's three hundred dollars in it for you."

Amused, the chopper pilot stared up at Herman and then, ignoring him, picked his 45 out from under his pillow and slipped it quickly into his shoulder holster.

"Listen, kid," Herman said, "that's a hundred dollars a minute."

He waited, while the pilot bent down and began lacing up his boots.

"Then you won't do it?" Herman said. The kid didn't bother to answer. "Look, it's no skin off your nose. Just take the chopper there, hand it through the window. Ten seconds. No one even has to get out. I radioed; they're expecting it. I mean, it's important. Tell you what, I'll make it four hundred."

The pilot straightened up, picked up his helmet off the bedpost, and tucked it up under his arm. "Three hundred a man," he said. "Three hundred for me; three hundred for the co-pilot; three hundred for the crew chief; three hundred for the door gunner."

Herman looked at him as if he were crazy.

"That's four hundred a minute," the pilot offered helpfully. "Your company can afford it."

"We're a construction firm," Herman said angrily. "Not diamond makers."

"You could fool me," the pilot said, ignoring him again while he fished for his flight glasses.

"Someone else will do it."

228

"Then find him," the pilot said. He left the engineer standing there in front of his cot and walked out of the hutch.

"Fucken kids," Herman mumbled under his breath as he picked up the box and walked out of the empty room into the sunlight. The 115-degree heat of Nam swirled suffocatingly around him. For a moment he closed his eyes. God, it gets hot, he thought. Walking across the company area, he paid no attention to the choppers starting up all around him. By the time he reached the gate, he was puffing and his white shirt was soaked.

"Well?"

"Well, what?" Herman asked, walking around the front of the company jeep.

"They wouldn't do it?"

"What the hell does it look like?" Herman said, dropping the box heavily onto the back seat.

Thompson moved the M-16 off the front seat to make room. "We told 'em we'd get it up to them."

Herman, giving Thompson a disgusted look, climbed in as the first gunship, turbine roaring, cleared the wire a few meters in front of them. Thompson waited until Herman could hear him.

"So," he said, leaning forward against the steering wheel, "what do we do now?"

"What?" Herman asked as a second gunship came whining out over them.

"What do we do now?" Thompson said louder. Herman waited until the chopper was gone.

"I offered him three hundred bucks and he so much as told me to get screwed. Three hundred, *three hundred!*"

"Maybe you should have offered him more," Thompson said, reaching for the starter.

Herman gave him a quick, angry look. "I didn't have to," he said, wiping the sweat off the back of his sunburned neck. "He told me he'd do it for twelve hundred dollars."

Thompson pursed his lips. "Hmmm," he said, tilting his head as he started the engine. "Bit steep, even for Nam." He was just putting the jeep into gear, when Herman stopped him.

"An idea?" Thompson asked, sitting back.

Herman picked up the box and climbed out of the jeep.

"Hey," Thompson said, "this time pick a kid that's just got over here, will you?"

Herman walked across the broken, dusty ground back into the compound. It was getting time to go, he thought. A third gunship careened out over his head. He held his breath against the noise and sudden down-draft, and then it was gone. Maybe if he'd go out in the field a few weeks and get back into some kind of shape, he'd be able to hack it better. The air conditioner was what was screwing him up. He had to do something, though. Thompson was getting on his nerves, and even his moose was beginning to annoy him. He walked right into the headquarters building. None of the guards challenged him or even asked what he was carrying. Nobody checked anything. It was almost as hot inside the building as out; all the windows were open. He walked up to the first desk.

"Can I help you?" The kid looked no older than the chopper pilot.

"I'd like to see Sergeant Kowlow. He was here last time I came by."

"Sergeant Kowlow?" The Corporal looked thoughtful for a moment. "Sorry, I don't think he's here; I mean, I've never heard of him."

"There might be a few sergeants around you haven't . . ." Herman was about to remind him again that maybe he didn't know everybody in the Army, when someone yelled from the back of the room.

"Hey, Cramer! Cramer!" The Corporal turned his head. "Better let the Old Man know that S-2 just called. Gunship and a loach got lit up near Qui Nhou."

The Corporal waved and turned back to Herman.

"I think Sergeant Kowlow DEROS'ed back to the States almost two months ago," he said.

"Who replaced him?"

"Sergeant Brown."

"Brown?" Herman thought for a second. "Thomas Brown?"

"Sorry," the Corporal shrugged. "I don't know what Sergeant Brown's first name is."

"Is he in?"

"He might be. His office is the first one on the right."

Herman turned away. Last year, he thought, as he walked sweating down the corridor. Even the money wouldn't make it worth another. He reminded himself to send part of this month's money to his second bank account. It was always good to be a little cautious. It wouldn't do for his and his wife's joint account to get too far out of hand.

He found Sergeant Brown in his office, sitting at his desk, a huge air conditioner blowing in over him.

"London . . . Herman London," Brown said good-naturedly. Herman nodded and walked into the room.

231

Brown, his wide face spread even wider, kept smiling, though he didn't bother to get up from behind his desk. They had met each other over a year ago when Herman was up in I Corps, building the harbor at Danang, and Brown was working in the NCO clubs. They had hardly known each other. Herman was impressed that Brown remembered.

"Your kids are getting a bit more hard-nosed than they used to be," Herman said wearily, putting the box down on the desk.

Brown stared at the box for a moment and then, motioning to the only other chair in the office, leaned back. "It's not '67," he said, taking two cigars out of his pocket. Herman wondered about his pallor, but then he could not remember ever seeing him suntanned, even down in I Corps.

"No thanks," Herman said, sitting down. The sweat was drying, making his clothes stick to him.

"I asked one of your pilots going up near Quin Yon to deliver that box to some of the boys working up near there, and he almost spit on me."

Lighting his cigar, Brown nodded sympathetically. "It's a different kind of war," he said matter-of-factly.

"What happened to Kowlow?"

"He wanted to get out. He'd had enough."

"How long was he here for?" Herman asked.

"A little over two years."

"NCO clubs the whole time?"

Brown shook his head. "No, the last year he was working with the PX's. Tape recorders, tape decks, turntables, that kind of thing."

"Almost as good as construction work," Brown said, giving Herman a small conspiratorial smile.

Herman let it go. "Do you think you could help me with that?" he asked, pointing toward the box. Brown put the cigar in the ashtray.

"I think so," he said, moving his chair closer to the desk. Herman reached into his shirt pocket for a cigarette.

"I offered the chopper pilot two hundred to take it up to Ton Bi."

"What's in it?" the Sergeant asked, sliding the box a bit closer to him.

"Couple of fifths of scotch. They ran out and they're having some kind of party up there tonight. They radioed down, and I promised I'd get it to them."

"Who's up there?" Brown said.

"Supervisors from AM and D. Doing some kind of on-site inspection."

"Ton Bi," the Sergeant said. "Hmmm, that's pretty far. . . . Well," he said, pushing back his chair, "I think I should be able to do something for you." He put his hands on his knees as if he were about to launch himself out of his seat. "What were you offering again?"

"Two . . . three hundred." Herman corrected.

"Good," Brown said, standing up. "Be right back."

"We'll have to wait a couple of minutes," he said when he returned to the office. "Don't worry. I'm sure it will be OK."

"Fine," Herman said, getting up. "Listen, I have a friend out near the gate; I'll tell him what's happening."

"Oh, London?"

"Yeah?"

Brown was still standing by the desk, next to the box. "Got any extra generators at your place? Not for good, just for three or four days?"

Herman could feel the heat from the corridor fighting to get past him into the room. "They're tough to get hold of. They power this whole damn country." He looked toward the big air-conditioning unit stuck into the window. "They're like gold, only worse."

Brown nodded soberly. "I really need one. I sort of promised . . . a real promise." He sat down on the desk. "I move a lot of stuff around here. It would be worth your while."

"OK," Herman said. "We can always have one break down and have to ship it somewhere to get it fixed. You do fix generators here."

Brown grinned. "We fix everything here."

Thompson was waiting for him inside the building. "A few more minutes," Herman said, walking up to him.

Thompson picked his rifle off the bench where he had laid it. "If we don't leave soon, we'll be riding back in the dark."

"Could be," Herman said.

"Look," Thompson said seriously, "you do stupid things around here and you're going to get yourself hurt. Just leave the booze. If they can get it out, fine; if not, we'll come back and pick it up tomorrow."

Herman checked his watch. "One minute," he said.

When he walked back into the office, Brown was on the phone. He motioned Herman into the office. "OK, yeah, sure; give me a call when it's loaded. And thanks, Grieley; it's really appreciated." He put down the phone. "It will go," he said, leaning back in his chair. "There's a lot of stuff happening up around Qui Nhou. We'll probably have to resupply before it gets dark."

"Sounds good," Herman said.

"Want something to drink?"

"No thanks," Herman said. "I just talked to my partner, and he wants to get back. If it would be OK, I'll leave the box. If you can get it out—fine. If you can't, we'll come by tomorrow and pick it up."

"Sure, anyway you want it."

"You know, Sarge, that wasn't the first pilot I tried. Just out of curiosity, how you gonna get it up to Bon Ti? Order one of 'em to take it?"

Brown looked amused. "If I did that, they'd break every bottle one by one." He reached for another cigar. "They'll do it, but they have to think it's worthwhile. I mean, they know where it's going and what's there."

"So?" Herman asked.

"So," Brown said, lighting his cigar, "I rewrap it, put some stickers on it, and it becomes penicillin, or plasma, or something." He took a few puffs. "How much did we agree on?"

"Three hundred," Herman said.

"We'll have to pass it around a bit." Herman remained mute. "Well," Brown added good-naturedly, "it'll have to do."

Herman took three hundred-dollar bills from his wallet and handed them to Brown.

"Thanks. Tell me," he said, "do they give you guys more for two-year contracts?"

"Yeah," Herman said.

Brown nodded approvingly. "Tax-free, too. Hmmm. With odds and ends I bet you could triple that base salary in two years."

"We work for it," Herman said, putting away his wallet. "Anyway, thanks for taking care of the liquor for me."

"That's OK," Brown said. "I'll be in touch."

It was only after Herman had left the room that Brown folded the money and put it into his own wallet.

"We should get out of this jungle war. With our fire power, if we were up against a regular army we'd wipe them out. But we're shooting at trees and bushes."

Trooper, 1st Air Cav
Surgical Ward
U.S. Army Hospital, Zama, Japan

16

Brock

You don't wear tiger stripes in Japan. They're not authorized. Jungle fatigues, regular fatigues, class-A khakis, summer or winter greens, even Army shorts are OK, but not tiger stripes. With their jagged slashes of black and green, it's hard to pass them off as being defensive. They're for the jungle, for tracking and killing without being seen. So to spare the sensitivities of our Japanese hosts, the United States Army had ruled that tiger stripes were not to be worn in that country. Every now and then, though, someone ignores the regulations. Usually, after a little official harassment, he gives in and takes them off. Some, though, don't. A few, simply because they've been through it all and don't give a shit; others, because even in Japan, their war's not over; some, a little of both. These are the ones you can't push around, and if you hassle them about anything—even their uniforms—you'd better be ready to go all the way, because they'll take you there whether you want to go or not.

Brock noticed the Major glaring at him, but kept right on walking.

"Hey you . . . you in the camies."

Camies . . . ! Camies . . . ? Jesus! Without turning around, Brock came slowly to a stop.

"Yes you, soldier."

Amused, Brock turned around.

"Come here!"

Smiling, Brock walked slowly back down the corridor. He was carrying his bush hat. His short blond hair had been bleached almost white by the sun, and he had the pinched, drawn look of having been outdoors too long. Except for his first lieutenant's bars and jump wings, there was nothing else on his tiger stripes, not even a unit patch.

"We don't wear that uniform around here," the Major said.

"But I'm not from around here," Brock said pleasantly enough.

"Where you from?"

"Sorry, can't tell you that."

"Sir," the Major corrected sharply. "What unit are you with?"

"Sorry, can't tell you that, either."

"What are you doing here?"

"I'm afraid I can't tell you that . . . sir."

The Major flushed.

"Lieutenant," he said angrily, "you're getting yourself into trouble."

Unmoved, Brock remained silent, offering nothing.

"Who's your commanding officer!"

"Right now," Brock said, turning to observe a patient being rolled past him, "I am."

"Lieutenant," the Major barked, his voice echoing up and down the corridor, "junior officers stand at attention when they are talking to their seniors."

With people stopping nearby, he was gathering himself to go on when Brock suddenly turned on him. His whole posture had changed. The calm indifference had vanished, and now the major found himself facing a cold furious young man.

"You!" Brock said contemptuously. "You, senior! A

240

hospital personnel officer." The change had been so abrupt, Brock's contempt so brazenly expressed, that for a moment the Major was startled.

"I want you in my office this afternoon," he stammered, his face purple with fury.

"I won't be there," Brock said quietly.

"You'll be there, dammit, and when you walk into my office, Lieutenant, I want you in class-A khakis, or you'll go back to Nam in cuffs. Understand?"

Brock didn't even bother to answer. He simply turned his back on the Major and continued on his way to the admissions office.

The med evacs had already come in for that day and the admissions clerk had just finished typing up the daily census when Brock walked into the office. Ignoring the Corporal's stare at his tiger stripes, he handed him a piece of paper. "Could you tell me if these men are still here?"

It is not uncommon for an officer if he is in Japan to visit his men. Almost all the wounded from Nam come there. What was uncommon was the Lieutenant's list. Everyone was ranger-qualified. Everyone was Special Forces. Each had graduated from Recondo School, spent time at the Royal Jungle Tracking School of Malaysia, had been HALO trained—and each had been shot. There was not a frag wound or booby-trap injury among them. In a hospital full of idiotic blunders, miscalculations, and stupid mistakes, it was an extraordinary group.

Brock did not stay long on the wards. His men—though surprised and obviously pleased to see him—were restrained, treating him with a reserve quite uncommon for a first lieutenant. He ignored their wounds, merely thanked them, offered his help if ever needed, and left. They assumed he was going back.

It was only in the intensive-care unit that his smooth routine faltered. Perhaps it was the shock of the room itself. After the drab, dimly lit green of the surgical and orthopedic wards, it was like suddenly turning a corner and walking into a sunspot. Brilliantly lit, with huge banks of overhead lights, spotless and shadowless, its gleaming tiled floors and walls glared at everyone who walked in.

The patients, brown and lean from Nam, lay naked in rows, with their wounds, chest tubes, and catheters exposed; some had their stumps up, oozing on blocks. Brock hesitated in the doorway.

"Yes?" the ward master asked, approaching him.

"Sergeant Ade," Brock said, his eyes searching the rows of wounded men.

"I'm sorry, sir, but he's critical."

"I know, but I haven't much time. I'd like to see him. He was part of my team."

The ward master looked at Brock's tiger stripes and bush hat. "OK, but put on one of those gowns."

Ade was at the far end of the room. Wearing a white surgical gown Brock walked down the center aisle, and the patients, sunken-eyed, emaciated, barely able to lift their heads, watched him as he passed—boys with amputated arms sewn closed with black thread, like the seams of a purse, kids with abdomens half open, draining pus into liter bottles. A nurse, adjusting an IV, looked up. The smell of sterile soap and rubber was everywhere.

242

He stopped by the foot of the last bed and waited for Ade to open his eyes, watching the blood dripping slowly out of the bottle into the catheter they had sewn into the patient's neck. When Ade finally looked up, it took him a while to focus his eyes.

"Made it, huh?" he whispered.

Brock moved closer to the side of the bed. "Yeah," he said. "Made it."

"Going back?"

"No." Brock shook his head. "They offered me another team, but . . . well, I didn't want to begin again. I'm going home."

"You're gonna be tough in the bars, man."

Brock smiled. "Yeah—guess so."

"Still having the same dream?"

"Same one," Brock said soberly. "Same one, every night."

Ade closed his eyes against the lights. "Should see somebody about it."

"Later. How they treating you?"

"I get all the blood I need."

The ward master was walking toward them.

"I've got to go," Brock said, taking Ade's limp hand in both of his. "I'll keep in touch. Good luck."

Ade looked up at him and smiled wanly. "That's past, man. Gone. Take care."

Brock was walking away even before the ward master reached him.

After lunch, the Major called the Far East Personnel

Center for the Lieutenant's records. There weren't any. An hour later, a colonel from G-4 headquarters, United States Army, Japan, called and asked, why the inquiry. The Colonel listened politely, told the Major to forget about it, and hung up.

That evening Brock threw away his tiger stripes. Before dark, he came to the hospital officers' club wearing class-A khakis and carrying a small flight bag. His jungle boots were gone, and in their place he was wearing gleaming jump boots. His short-sleeve shirt was ironed; his pants, spotless and creased, were bloused perfectly into his boots. Under his combat infantry badge and jump wings, he wore his ribbons, three rows of them—the Distinguished Service Cross, the Silver Star, the Bronze Star, the deep purple of the Purple Heart, and the Vietnamese Ranger Ribbon. The others—the National Defense Ribbon, the Vietnam Campaign Ribbon, and the Vietnam Service Ribbon—the foolish little everyman medals— had been left off.

He put his case in the coat room and walked into the lounge. It wasn't much of a place—a bar, linoleum flooring, a few tables and chairs, and a juke box. It had been opened as a place for hospital patients and on-duty personnel, and being removed from the main Army base, without any colonels or colonels' wives to be concerned, it had all the aspects of a sleazy southern bar. But after Nam it was enough, and as early as it was, the lounge was already fairly crowded.

Brock took off his cap and walked quietly past the soldiers at the bar. Some of them, catching sight of his ribbons, stopped talking as he came by. An infantry captain, who had been standing near the bar when he walked in, approached his table at the back of the room.

"How about a drink?"

Brock looked up. "No, thanks," he said.

"Come on, I'm buying—anything you like."

"Nothing, really."

"Gin and tonic!" the Captain said, snapping his fingers, and without waiting for Brock to protest, he walked with a slight limp back to the bar. In a few minutes he was back, carrying two glasses. "Here you are, Lieutenant."

"Thanks." Brock put his glass down beside his cap.

The Captain sat down and looked at his ribbons. "Winning the war yourself, Lieutenant?" he said, taking a sip of his drink.

"Part," Brock said. He summoned the waiter.

"Which part is that?"

"A glass of milk, please," Brock said to the waiter. He turned back to the Captain. "My part."

"From the looks of it, everyone else's too."

"No, just mine."

"You know," the Captain said, pointing to the untouched glass, "that's pretty good gin."

"I'm sure it is," Brock said, paying the waiter, "but I had hepatitis."

"Delta?"

"No."

"North?"

"Yeah," Brock said whimsically, "way north."

"What unit were you with?"

"None."

"Rangers, eh?" the Captain persisted.

"Sort of." The juke box started blaring. Annoyed, Brock looked over his shoulder.

"Were you an LRRP?"

"No," Brock said. "We worked too far north for that." He reached into his shirt pocket for a cigarette, and the Captain leaned over the table to light it for him.

"Yes, that's quite an array of ribbons," the Captain said.

"Let's talk about you," Brock said.

"I was an FO for the 25th."

"Tracks?"

"Yeah."

"Fat. That's real fat."

"Sometimes," the Captain said.

"At least you always have enough water. How many gallons does each one of those damn things carry?"

"Thirty . . . sometimes fifty," the Captain said, grabbing his leg to help straighten it.

"You know," Brock said, "I can remember once, getting back below the DMZ—you get real freaky after you've been out a while—and the first Americans we ran into coming out of the DMZ were a track squadron, a couple of APC's, and a track. I just couldn't believe how much water they had. I mean, I just stood there and couldn't believe it. We'd been chewing bamboo shoots for almost a week, and before that, for two weeks, we'd been drinking anything—rain water, river shit, stuff right out of the paddies. And then we came out, and the first thing I saw was these guys standing by their damn tracks spilling water all over. I could have killed them," he said solemnly; "I swear to God I would have, too, if my men hadn't . . ."

"I didn't know we had units up there in North Vietnam."

"We do," Brock said.

"Hmmm. ..." The Captain looked unconvinced.

"You think the whole fucken war is fought with APC's
and tanks?"

"No. I just didn't think we had ground units working
up there. I figured the photograph planes took care of
that."

"We're there," Brock said coldly, signaling the waiter
again.

"How long were you up there?" the Captain asked.

"A long time."

"A year?"

"We'd go up on missions."

The Captain waited for him to go on, but Brock just sat
there thoughtfully, pushing the ashtray around. The
room was filling up. Despite the crowd, it was not a
very loud place. Most of the men were just standing
around talking or drinking quietly by themselves. A few
were leaning awkwardly on their crutches. Three or four
were still in shoulder casts and arm braces, while others
were wearing surgical packs.

"How did you get into it?"

"Happened. I majored in Chinese in college, and somebody found out. They're very good at that—must have a
line on everybody. Anyway, they called me at the beginning of my senior year. I said no, but a year later my
brother was killed in Nam and I said yes."

"And they sent you to Nam?" the Captain asked, pointing to the Airborne cap on the table.

247

"No." Brock was about to go on when a tray of dishes crashed behind him. He jumped in his chair and turned sharply, tensed, his face hard in the dim light. He was almost on his feet before he caught himself. Disgusted, he settled back in his seat. His hand shook as he reached for another cigarette.

The captain slid his lighter across the table. "You were saying you didn't go to Nam."

"Do you know anything about the Special Forces?" Brock asked. "I was with an SMT group—Special Mission Team. After jump school and Ranger training, my team was sent to Malaysia—the Royal British Jungle Tracking School there. They'd send us out in that jungle and then capture us and beat us up and then send us out again. I thought we were tough, too—Airborne, Ranger training, Special Forces school—but they knew how to live in the jungle, how to use it. For Christ's sake, they even liked it." He picked up the captain's lighter and turned it over and over in his hand. "That's what we learned, all six of us—how to live there, like it was home."

"Can I sit down?"

The Captain looked up over his shoulder at the trooper. "Sure," he said, motioning to the chair beside him.

It took the soldier a little while to lower himself into the seat. "Sorry," he said. "I can't bend too well yet. Round sort of bounced off my backbone. At least that's what the surgeon said."

"You're lucky," Brock said. "Since the bombing halt, the VC and NVA have been moving tons of new weapons into the South. They're all carrying brand new chicon Soviet block weapons now, AK's, Simonov carbines, RP-

46's, RPD light machine guns. You were really lucky. You must have got hit with an old FN or carbine. A round from one of their new weapons would've broken you in two. Sure it wasn't a frag?"

"I don't know," the trooper said. "It was almost dark. Nearly everyone in my platoon was killed." Brock, about to interrupt, stopped himself. "It could have been a frag; hell, it could have been a piece of an A-bomb for all I know. God knows there was enough shit going off."

"How come you all got killed?" Brock asked quickly.

"We got caught."

"Nobody gets caught."

"*We* did."

"You don't get caught," Brock repeated. "You just fuck up."

"We didn't fuck up," the trooper said stubbornly, shifting his weight in the chair, "we got caught."

"It's all the same."

"Look!" He stared angrily at Brock, then turned to the Captain, "We were coming back through an area the ARVN's had just swept. We were almost home. They let the point and the slack through and got the rest of us boxed in. Then they popped their claymores. It didn't matter where we moved, they had us. Everybody was hit or dead in the first thirty seconds." He turned back to Brock. "You know, we didn't try to get ambushed."

"Nobody does," Brock said, looking at his watch.

"Wait a minute," the Captain said, "that's not really fair."

"Fair?" Brock looked amused. "No," he said, "I guess it's not. How were you moving, soldier?"

"What do you mean?"

"Were you in a traveling overwatch, in column, squads flanking? Were you coming back through one of the ways you had gone out?"

"Column."

"And you were almost home?"

The trooper nodded. A few fellows from the nearby tables had gathered around to listen.

"We weren't cherries, man," the trooper said drily. "They'd have had anyone. There was no way out. It was an X ambush. Once you're in it—you're in it." He looked at Brock's ribbons. "You must know that."

"There is only one way to move through the jungle," Brock said. "The point takes everything out in front of him, the whole 180 degrees, not the overhead, just eye level, and below. The slack takes the left overhead and the 90 degrees to his right. The third man takes the left overhead and the 90 degrees to his left. The fourth man takes the area to his side and the overhead to his right. The fifth, the area to his side and the overheads. The last man covers the rear and, if he has to, cleans the track. And," he went on slowly, almost pedantically, "you walk carefully, at a British slow march, putting your foot down slowly, stopping every five or ten meters. I know," he said, stopping the interruption. "But that's the way it has to be done or you get caught. Even . . ." he went on slowly, looking across at the trooper, "even if you don't want to. You get a feeling then, when you move like that—a rhythm. You know when there's something up there, when something is wrong. Little sounds, mostly."

"Did you rotate points?" asked a patient who was wearing Airborne and Ranger patches on his uniform.

Brock looked up but seemed reluctant to go on.

"Did you rotate points?" the Ranger asked again, a bit louder. The conversation at the surrounding tables stopped.

"No," Brock said.

"I'm sorry, Lieutenant," the soldier said, "you'll have to speak louder, I got my ears fucked up, too."

"No," Brock said louder. "But we never left him alone out there, either. When our point saw something and knew he'd been seen, he'd fall backwards, firing off single rounds. The slack, even if he didn't see anybody, would step forward and spray the same area with automatic fire. By the time he was out of ammunition, the point had his weapon reloaded and was firing again. Most of the time, though, we saw 'em first and just moved away."

"But companies aren't six men," someone volunteered. He was wearing a shoulder cast, with his fingers in steel traction.

"The New Zealanders do fine," Brock said, "and so do the Australians."

"They're all volunteers."

Brock looked coldly at the soldier who had just spoken. "Tell that to the draftees who get killed," he said. "I'm sure they'd love to know."

"How the hell did that happen, then?" a soldier asked, pointing at Brock's Purple Heart ribbon. "I mean, if you know how to live in the jungle so well."

Brock, acting as if he hadn't heard, slowly, in a very

stylized way, picked up the Captain's lighter in front of him and lit another cigarette. The trooper was just beginning to look triumphant when the captain asked, "Where were you when it happened?"

"Haiphong," Brock said, putting the lighter back exactly where it had been before.

The soldier looked surprised. "Haiphong? Did you jump in?"

"No. We walked."

"What did you do for supplies?" asked a soldier with a surgical patch over one eye.

Brock shrugged. "Mercenaries—agents, traitors, whatever you want to call them. They put out caches for us."

"Can you trust 'em?"

"No, you can't trust anybody. They put out two or three for every one we needed. When you get to the one you'll use, you're just careful. You stake it out for half a day, and if anything looks foolish, you just pass it up." He crushed out his half-smoked cigarette. "On one mission, we had to pass up three and just keep going with what we had. We ended up living on rats and chocolate bars and stealing ammunition from the gooks. Anyway, we fucked up. We didn't get caught. We were on a mission, when an Air Force colonel got shot down. Some fool in Washington decided that my team should go get him. We had to break our routine and travel during the day to get there."

"Did you get him?"

"No, we got there a little after the NVA. I wasn't going to lose my team. They had him, they could keep him."

252

Brock looked at his watch again. "I've got to go," he said, reaching for his cap.

"Just one thing," the Ranger said. "Why do you think you learned so much more in Malaysia than we did in Ranger training and Special Forces school? I mean, maybe you got better at what you knew, but as for learning more . . ."

"It's not what you know," Brock said. "It's a feeling you get. Like tracking. You need it when you're alone and on your own in the jungle. There's no one to help you out there. When you get good, you can find a track and tell not only how many they are, but their morale, how far they're going to go, whether they're near their camp, the weapons they're carrying. We found a Viet Cong hospital complex the Special Forces had been walking over for days . . ."

"How can you tell their weapons," a soldier asked, "and how far they're going?"

"From the imprints when they put them down to rest. Their morale from the way they drag their feet, or the joints that may be lying around. If they're near a base camp, they wouldn't be conserving their food; they'll be throwing it away half-eaten. If the branches are broken along the track at shoulder height, they're carrying their weapons at port arms. They're waiting then, expecting. If the branches aren't broken, their weapons are slung. But," he went on quickly, "all this is just technique. There is a feeling that you get after a while—that's what's important," Brock said, picking up his hat and playing with it. "We were going through a village once. We were look-

253

ing for a certain party. We took off our boots and walked into each hut. It was midnight. I went into three like that and suddenly realized I'd gone into each hut the same way—standing up—so the next one I went in on my belly. An RPD burst took out the door a bit above my head." He stopped and shrugged, "Things like that. . . . Well," he said, pushing back his chair, "got to go home."

"I'll walk you out," the Captain said. "Where you going now?" he asked as they left the room.

"Fort Gordon for a while. My flight bag's in there—" Brock pointed to the coat room—"and then home."

The Captain waited while Brock walked in to get his bag. He hadn't noticed the scar, red and raw, that came up across the back of the lieutenant's neck.

"No, no," Brock said when the Captain offered to carry his flight bag. "It's OK, I can carry it. I should use this shoulder anyway."

They walked outside into the warm Japanese night. There was no moon. The fuzzy red lights of the hospital's helipad blinked at them from across the open field. The captain pulled out a cigarette and reached into his pocket for his lighter. Even as it sparked into flame, Brock swung around and knocked it out of his hand. Sputtering, it hit the ground and went out. There was an embarrassed silence.

"It's all right, Lieutenant," the Captain said, bending to pick it up. "There's no one out there any more."

"If there is any blessing in being there
it is in the shortness of things.
There is no wasting away there, no
philosophical concerns about medical
ethics, about pulling out the plugs and
turning off the machines. When they die
there they die straight out, right off
the choppers. It's sort of clean work.
No brain tumors to worry about, no
chronic renal disease, no endless dialysis,
no multiple sclerosis, no leukemics—
and no goddamn families to have to
worry about."

Battalion surgeon, 101st Airborne
R and R
U.S. Army Hospital, Zama, Japan

17

I Don't Want to
Go Home Alone

EDWARDS picked up the stethoscope from his desk. "Look," he said, "you can say what you want about the Army and its problems, but I learned this much from going home: the Army treats you better dead than alive. I know," he added quickly to keep the Captain from talking. "I know, it was my fault. I shouldn't have got involved with taking the body back. But I did."

"It's coming," the corpsman said, stepping away from the window.

Edwards stuffed the stethoscope into his back pocket. "OK. Tell the ward master. How many did they say?"

The Captain put his half-finished cup of coffee on the desk. "One VSI and one SI."

Edwards nodded and then, as if he'd just remembered something, checked his watch against the clock over the door.

"The States are sixteen hours behind us," the Captain offered.

"In time, maybe." Edwards pulled his lab coat off the rack. "Better fill the whirlpools. I'll be down at the landing pad."

In the dimly lit corridor he looked again at his watch. Sixteen hours. It would be eighteen for Nam. What difference did it make, eighteen or a million? He pushed open the double doors to the burn unit.

The huge overhead lights were off, leaving only the night lights to flicker feebly across the shiny tiled floor. He walked quietly down the center aisle of the ward, his footsteps echoing lightly ahead of him. The beds lining the wall were barely visible, the patients no more than lumps against the frames. From the far end of the ward came the faint mechanical hissing of a respirator. He stopped a moment near one of the steel arched Stryker frames to listen. The machine's slow, regular rhythm was almost soothing. How many times he'd heard it before. Someone had said he'd signed more death certificates than any other doctor in Japan. Probably right, he thought, continuing on his way. At Kishine, the respirator was the sound of death, not life; in all his time there, he could not think of one patient who had got off the thing.

"Hi, Doc."

"Oh, Crowley," Edwards said, coming to a halt near the little cubicle at the back of the ward. "Sorry, I didn't see you in the dark."

The side curtain had been partially pulled. Stretched out on the bed, barely lit by the dials of the respirator, was a shadowy form.

"How's he doing, Sergeant?" Edwards asked the ward master, who was standing at attention by the machine that was slowly, insistently hissing air into and out of the charred body.

"Not too good, sir."

"What's his temperature?"

"Hundred and five. It was a hundred and seven before we put him on the cooling blanket."

"Blood cultures growing out anything?"

"Yes, sir; the lab called back tonight—Pseudomonas pseudomallei. Major Johnson put him on IV chloromycetin and tetracycline."

Edwards bent over to look more closely at the restrained body spread-eagled across the frame. The air smelled

258

sweet, like a dying orchard. "When did he come in?" he asked, peering at the grotesquely crusted body. Even the tips of his toes and fingers were charred and oozing; nothing had been spared.

"Four days after you left. Seventy percent second-degree and 15 percent third. At least Major Johnson thought it was second-degree, but it's beginning to look like it's all third."

Edwards examined the crust about the boy's swollen neck and chest. It had a sick metallic green cast to it. "When did he go sour?"

"He was doing fine until this morning. We had to give him Demerol every time he went into the whirlpool, but he's very hard-core. Nice kid. Then yesterday, he became confused and agitated. On the night shift his temp spiked, and he became unconscious. The surgeons trached him today, and Dr. Johnson put him on the respirator this evening."

Edwards sighed and stepped back from the bed. "How old?"

"What?"

"How old was he?"

Surprised, Crowley reached for the chart.

"Never mind," Edwards said. "Forget it."

"Sir."

"Yes?"

"You're sort of short now, aren't you?"

"Five months."

"That's not long."

"No," Edwards said absently, "no, it's not long."

"The evacs should be in soon."

"Yeah, that's where I'm going. I'll check on him later."

"No need, sir, you'll have your hands full. I'll have you called if anything changes."

As he walked away, Edwards could hear Crowley drawing the curtains closed behind him. The stairwell was empty, and he walked slowly down to the first floor and out onto the concrete walkway.

It was summer outside, and the night was as warm as indoors. He cut across the empty, silent field separating the hospital's squat buildings from the helipad, where the red lights of the landing strip flickered softly in the misty dark. Far away he heard the muffled, dull thudding of the chopper whopping its way through the heavy air, and suddenly he felt alone and desperately tired.

"Gentlemen: You have been assembled here at Yokota Air Base to escort these bodies home to the continental United States. Each body in its casket is to have, at all times, a body escort. Those caskets on the plane that do not at the present time have an escort will have them assigned at Oakland. Whatever the case, no casket will be allowed to leave the Oakland area without a proper escort. Escort duty is a privilege as well as an honor. An effort has been made to find an escort whose personal involvement with the deceased or presence with the family of the deceased will be of comfort and aid. Your mission as a body escort is as follows: to make sure that the body is afforded, at all times, the respect due a fallen soldier of the United States Army. Specifically it is as follows: 1) To check the tags on the caskets at every point of departure.

2) To insist, if the tags indicate the remains as non-view-able, that the relatives not view the body. Remember that non-viewable means exactly that—non-viewable. . . ."

Grimly, with the chopper coming nearer—louder— Edwards walked up a slight rise, past a small, dimly lit sign:

KISHINE BARRACKS
109th UNITED STATES ARMY HOSPITAL
United States Army, Japan
Burn Unit

"Coastal Airlines loads the bodies on an angle. Be sure that if the body you are escorting is being carried by Coastal Airlines that the caskets are loaded head down: this will keep the embalming fluid in the upper body. If the body is loaded incorrectly, namely, feet down, the embalming fluid will accumulate in the feet and the body may, under appropriate atmospheric conditions, begin to decompose."

By the time he reached the evac area, the floodlights were on and the chopper had landed. Coming in from the dark around the back of the evac building Edwards was dazzled by the sudden lights. The Huey, low and glistening, its rotors still whirling, sat like a toy exactly in the middle of the arc lights. Its crew chief and co-pilot were already in the open hatchway unstrapping the litters from their carrying hooks. Edwards watched unseen while the corpsmen hurried out to the chopper to off-load the patients. The choppers usually came in about ten in the morning, but when a bad burn was evac'ed to Japan, they were flown in the same night. Burns are a very special kind of wound, and no physician anywhere wants the responsibility of caring for them, not even for a little while. For openers, burns look bad and the patients die.

"Each of the next of kin as listed in the deceased 201 file has already been visited by a survivor assistance officer. This was done in person by an officer in uniform from the nearest Army unit. Every effort is made to pick an officer from a similar racial and economic background. These families have already been convinced of the death by either the presentation of personal effects or the relating of an eye-witness report from a member of the deceased's unit. You need not convince the deceased's relatives. The point to remember is that the survivor assistance officer has been there before you and the next of kin have already accepted the death."

He was standing in the reflected glare of the landing lights, with the windy noise of the chopper rushing past him.

"Sir. Sir?" One of the corpsmen was shouting above the whining of the motor. "One of 'em's got a head wound, the other is just burned."

"Call the neurosurgeon," Edwards shouted back. He gave the empty chopper one more look and then followed the medic into the air evac area. By the time he reached the building, the medics had placed the two litters on the movable stretcher racks and one of them, working on the patient nearest the door, was already setting up an IV.

"He's OK, Major," the air-evac Sergeant said. "The head injury's over there."

"One hundred and seventy," the corpsman said as Edwards approached the litter. The wounded soldier, his head wrapped, was lying unconscious on his back, with the blood pressure cuff still wrapped around his arm.

"Expecting trouble, Tom?"

"Well, sir, I figured I'd leave the cuff on. He don't look too good."

"I'll give you that," Edwards said. He began to unwrap the gauze from around the patient's head. The boy was breathing; other than that, he looked dead. Edwards pinched his neck, but there was no response. As he unwound the gauze it became wet and then blood-soaked. Now he was down to the four-by-four surgical pads, and finally to the wound itself. Carefully he lifted up the last pack. Despite himself, he closed his eyes.

"He's 47-percent burned," the Sergeant said, reading the cover sheet of the soldier's medical record. "Took an AK round a little in front of the right eye. Removed the right eye, traversed the left orbit, removing the left eye, and came out near the left temple, apparently blowing out the left side of his head."

"Don't worry. I'll be careful, Bob. Honest, I'll be careful..."

263

"Send him to neurosurgery," Edwards said. "We'll treat his burns up there."

"An IV?"

"No, just send him up."

He walked across to the other wounded trooper. The corpsman had just got the IV started.

"Sorry it took so long, sir," he said. "Hard to find a vein."

The boy was awake, nervously looking at the needle the corpsman had stuck into the back of his hand.

"Hi," Edwards said. "How do you feel?"

The soldier looked up at him apprehensively. The skin on his face had been seared red and all his hair and eyebrows and lashes had been burned away.

"I know you're nervous," Edwards said soothingly. "Just try to relax. I'm the chief of the burn unit. I'll be your doctor for a while until you get better." As he pulled back the blanket the soldier grimaced. "Sorry," he said, lifting the cover more carefully.

The burns, red and raw, ran the whole charred length of the boy's body. Unconsciously Edwards began adding up the percentages of burned area, tallying them in his mind. He suddenly realized what he was doing and, for a moment, as he stood there staring at the burns, he looked stricken. "How did it happen?" he asked gently, carefully dropping back the covers.

"I . . . I was carrying detonators . . ."

"Dear Bob: We are fighting very hard now. I haven't written Mom and Dad about it. I don't want to worry

them. But we are getting hit and badly. I'm the only lieutenant in the company who hasn't been hit yet. And last week I lost two RTO's. They were standing right next to me. It gets a bit spooky. I know what you said about my flack vest, but you haven't been here and you just don't know how hot it can get. On the move, it's just too damn heavy. You can't carry a 60-pound rucksack in 110-degree heat and an 11-pound flack vest. I make the point wear his, but then someone else carries his gear. It's like your complaint about patients demanding penicillin—sometimes you just can't use it. It's the same with a flack vest. Besides, it wouldn't stop a round, and that's what we've been getting lately. But I'll wear it when I can. By the way, you're beginning to sound like Mom. About what's been happening lately. I'm not complaining, don't get the wrong idea. There is, honestly, something very positive about being over here. I can see it in myself and my men. Not the war itself, God knows that's hopeless enough, but what happens to you because of it. I'll never be the same again. I can feel myself growing. Unfortunately you only see one end of it. That's a bit sad, because there are other endings and even middles. A lot of guys get out of here OK, and despite what they say, they're better for it. I can see it in myself. I'm getting older over here in a way that I never could at home or maybe anywhere. For the first time in my life, everything seems to count. All the fuzziness is gone, all the foolishness. I can't believe the things that used to bother me, or even that I thought were important. You really see yourself over here. It works on you, grinds you down, makes you better. Got to go: Thanks for the R and R. Say Hi to all the guys in the burn unit."

265

"What?" Edwards asked.

"Detonators. I must have taken a round in my ruck-sack. They just blew up, and then I was on fire. Tried to tear my gear off, but my hands . . ."

"It's all right," Edwards said. The evac Sergeant handed him the patient's medical jacket. Quickly turning the pages, he read: "Eighty percent second-degree and third degree. Debridged under general anesthesia at the 60 evac, Chu Ci. Six liter plasmonate . . . catheterized . . . furacin and sterile dressings . . . Demerol . . . 64-mg. q three hours." He looked at the cover sheet. "David Jen-sen, MOS B11; 1/30 E-2, 4th Division, 20 years old."

"Twenty years old," he thought, handing back the chart. "Grant's age."

"David," he said wearily.

"Yes, sir?"

"I'm going to have the corpsman take you to the ward."

"Yes, sir."

"The first thing we're going to do is put you in a whirl-pool bath to soak off your badages and remove what dead skin we can. It's going to hurt."

"Yes, sir," David said, his voice wavering.

"If it hurts, just let us know. Is that understood?"

"Yes, sir."

"You don't have to call me sir."

"Yes, sir; thank you, sir."

"Take him to C-4," Edwards said to the corpsman. "Tell Sergeant Dorsey I'll be right there. And David . . ."

"Yes, sir."

"Burns look and feel a lot worse than they are. You're going to get better."

266

"Yes, sir."

Edwards watched the corpsman wheel the boy out of the evac area and then left the area himself to go to the neurosurgery ward. It was a long walk. Like all Army hospitals, Kishine is fantastically spread out, its buildings and wards acres apart so that no one shell or bomb can get it all. By the time he got to the ward, the neurosurgeon was already in the treatment room. The patient, partially hidden by the nurse and doctor, was lying naked on the treatment table. There were blood-soaked clothes and bandages all over the floor. Cramer turned his head for a moment, looked at Edwards, and went back to work.

"His frontal lobe is torn up," Cramer said. "I'm going to have to take him up to the operating room and save what I can. What do you think about his burns?"

Looking over Cramer's shoulder Edwards saw that the surgeon's fingers were deep inside the half shell of the boy's skull. "Don't worry about the burns," he said, turning to leave.

"Oh, Edwards," Cramer said as he reached the door. "I know how close you two'd become. I'm sorry."

"Regardless of the branch of service: The emblem of the Infantry, crossed rifles, will be carried on every coffin. The deceased, where the remains are viewable, will be buried in full military uniform. The emblems on his uniform will be that of the service to which he was attached at the time of his death."

He walked down the corridor to the elevator. Leaning wearily against the wall, he pressed the button, and without looking, stepped in even as the door was opening, almost colliding with one of the patients. "Sorry," he said, moving over to the other side of the elevator. The patient, his bathrobe slung over his good shoulder—the other was wrapped in a plaster cast—smiled politely and was about to look away when he saw the doctor's name plate on his uniform.

"Excuse me, sir."

"Yes?"

"Do you have any relatives in Nam?"

"Yes," Edwards said, "I do."

"First Air Cav?"

"Yes."

"Is his name Grant?"

Edwards nodded as the elevator suddenly slowed to a stop.

"Your brother?" The door opened. "I thought so," the trooper said, obviously pleased. "You sort of look like him."

"Come on," Edwards said pleasantly, holding the door.

"I saw him about three weeks ago. There isn't a better platoon leader in the whole cav. But I can tell you this, they were handing him some shit to do, when I saw him. His unit was on their way to getting their ass whipped."

"Are you sure, Grant? Why don't you go into Tokyo? You only have a few days for your R and R. You might as well have a good time."

"But I want to see what you're doing."

"It's not nice."
"And where do you think I've been?"

He had been surprised at how well Grant had handled himself in the burn unit. He had seen more than one visitor walking through the ward trying desperately to be natural, moving stiffly from bed to bed, smiling and talking as if the boys weren't burned at all. When Grant visited, there were two ghastly 90-percent burns stretched out, blistered and dying on their Stryker frames. Grant had stopped to talk to them and stayed with each much longer than he had to. He was very much at ease. He didn't ignore their wounds, or pretend not to see they were so obviously dying. He simply talked to them, interestedly and honestly, with a concern so palpable that no one could doubt his sincerity. He was one of them and, for a moment, watching his brother sitting by their frames, Edwards felt suddenly very much outside it all. He was very proud of his younger brother.

"I've seen worse, Bob. Really . . . a lot worse."

"Sir?"
"Yes, I know," Edwards said gently. "They did get whipped."
When he got back to the burn unit, he found David in the treatment area, already floating full length in one of the whirlpool baths, his head supported on a padded

board to keep it above the waterline, the water gently churning about his burnt body. His IV bottle, hanging from a ceiling hook, was still working. A few of the dressings had already soaked off, and the medic was picking them out of the water. Taking an admissions chart off the wall rack, Edwards sat down on a chair next to the huge tub.

"OK?" he asked.

David, clenching his teeth, nodded.

"Just try to relax. I have a few things to ask you." He quickly went over what had happened, the illnesses that David had had, whether he had taken his CP pills, whether he was on any medicines. While he was taking the history, he carefully, in a pre-printed outline of a man that was drawn on the admissions sheet, sketched in the areas of the burns and their depth, using red for third degrees and blue for second; he kept filling in until almost the whole figure, front and back, was covered.

"David," he said, "we're going to debride you a bit— take off the dead skin. We are going to have to do it every day, a little bit at a time. That way it won't be as painful." David was looking anxiously at him. "Once you know what's going on, it won't be so bad. We're going to put you into the whirlpool every day, and all the skin that is loose, or loosening, is going to be removed. It has to be done." He hesitated a moment and then went on matter-of-factly. "If we don't take it off, it just stays and decays, forming a place for bacteria to grow and divide, and you'll just get infected. That's what we want to avoid, because if the burns get infected no new skin will form. It's going to hurt, and I'll give you something for the pain when I think you need it."

"Yes, sir."

"I've been doing this a long time, David, and I know when it really hurts and when it doesn't. We're going to have to be doing this for some time and we don't want to make an addict out of you, so we're only going to use the pain medicine when we have to. I know you can do it. There have been a lot of troopers, just like you, through here, and I know you're as fine as they are."

David had been staring up at him the whole time. What was left of his lips were clamped tight against the pain of the water churning against his blistered skin. "Yes, sir," he said, his voice trembling.

"OK, John," Edwards said. David looked nervously from him to the corpsman. Pieces of dead skin were already floating free. The corpsman, kneeling down beside the tub, began picking off those pieces that were still attached but had been loosened. "How long have you been in Nam, David?"

"Five . . . five months," David said, watching the corpsman pick a chunk of skin off his chest. He had to tug to get it off. David grimaced, barely suppressing a groan.

"How do you like the Vietnamese women?" the medic asked.

"Don't know," David said, painfully engrossed in watching the corpsman go after another piece of his skin. "Didn't meet any gooks."

"How come?" the medic asked, scooping a piece of skin out of the water.

"We killed 'em all."

Suddenly David let out a scream, and the scream, echoing off the spotless tile walls, pierced Edwards to his heart. His eyes clenched tight, the boy was fighting valiantly for control. Blood began oozing from the new patch of raw skin on his chest, and Edwards could see the tears rolling down his burned cheeks.

"Where you from, Doc?" the cab driver asked.

"Japan."

"Oh," the cabbie said, pulling away from the curb. "Thought so, saw the Fuji patch on your sleeve. Nice place, huh?"

"No," Edwards said.

"I heard that Japan was paradise."

"I work in a burn unit."

"Oh, get many burns over there?"

"There's a war on. Remember?"

"You mean, you get those guys in Japan?"

"Yeah," Edwards said. "We get those guys . . ."

"Major, Major?"

Edwards opened his eyes. It was the ward master.

"Excuse me, sir. Those flights back from the States are tough. I'm sure you haven't caught up with the time change. Why don't you take a sleeping pill and get some rest?"

"Think I'll take your advice," Edwards said, closing his clipboard. He wrote a Demerol order for David and then went to his room. As tired as he was, though, he couldn't sleep. Every time he drifted off, he'd see Grant's tag: "Remains, non-viewable." And all that time in the States he thought he could handle it.

He woke up in the morning exhausted, put on his wrinkled uniform, and went to the ward.

Johnson was already in the office. "Hi," he said, turning around from his desk. "You know you didn't have to work today—or yesterday, for that matter."

"I know." Edwards hung up his jacket. "There's really not much else to do."

Both he and Johnson had shared the same office for almost a year now. Johnson had been the plastic surgeon working with the burn unit at Duke University. He had been drafted and assigned to Kishine.

"You want to go on rounds?" Edwards asked.

Johnson pressed the button on the intercom. "Julian, we're gonna start rounds." He pushed himself away from the desk. "Let's go."

"How's the fellow on the respirator?"

"He died this morning," Johnson said, picking up his notes. "I told the corpsman to leave you alone."

They walked down the ward, stopping at each bed. Fifty-percent burns, 80-percent burns, hand burns, half-burned, arm burned, 70-percent burned, third-degree, first-degree, second-degree, pseudomonas infections, staphylococci infections, split thickness graphs, full thickness grafts, swing flaps, corneal burns, esophageal burns, tracheal burns, contractures, isolated tendon repairs, urinary tract infections, open wounds, closed wounds, furacin dressings; sulfamyalon, penicillin, chloromycetin, actino-

273

mycin D, renal failure, congestive heart failure, gram negative shock, steroids, isoprel, epinephrine, full diet, soft diet, liquid diet, hyperalimentation, normal saline, plasmonate, albumin, blood-type A, type O; unmatched, matched, cross-matched. . . .

"Your grafts are holding up nicely, Harold."

"Sergeant, increase Dermitt's Demerol to q three hours, prn."

"Let me see Denton's temp sheet."

"How's Leon's titers?"

"Robinson, you're doing fine."

"Jergons, I want you to do more P.T. with that hand."

They moved on down the ward. On each bed or posted on the wall above the frames were the patches of the units each patient belonged to: the yellow and black of the 1st Air Cav; the red and blue eagle of the 101st Airborne; the 25th Division, the 9th, the big red one of the 1st and the Americal—even the unconscious patients had their service identification. There was a 1st Air Cav patch over David's frame.

"You worked him up?" Johnson asked, taking David's chart out of the rack.

"Yeah," Edwards said, looking at the Ranger patch that someone had placed below the Cav emblem. "Eighty-percent second or third." Johnson put down the chart, and they moved on.

After rounds, Edwards had the ward master take down all the unit patches. "Sergeant, I don't care what you think about morale. They're out of the war now, and I want those damn playthings off the walls. That's an order. Off the walls."

He went down to the bacteriology lab and then to his office. Johnson had gone to X ray to check on a few films. He sat down at his desk and looked at the two weeks' accumulation of correspondence that had been piled neatly at the corner of his desk. He was reaching for the first letter when the phone rang.

"Major Edwards, this is Captain Eden. There are two generals who will be visiting Kishine today. The Colonel wanted me to make sure you'll be free to take them around."

"What time?" Edwards asked, balancing the phone on his shoulder while he read a letter.

"We're not sure."

"I'm afraid I'll be busy this afternoon. You'd better tell the Commander to take them through Kishine's pride and joy himself." Without waiting for an answer, he hung up.

The intercom was buzzing. "Major, Jensen's in the whirlpool."

"OK, be right there; thanks."

David was already in the tub, being debrided. Edwards knelt down by the side of the tub and checked the burns. At some places, on the thighs and chest, he could see down to the muscle fibers crisscrossing under the burned fat. "David, I'm going to stop your IV," he said, straightening up. "You're going to have to start eating. The ward master told me you didn't touch your breakfast. Hurt?"

Chewing on what remained of his lips, David winced.

"Jessie, why don't you give him twenty-five of Demerol."

"Yes, sir," the corpsman said.

"Why didn't you eat?"

"No one was there to feed me," David said, watching

the corpsman open the medicine cabinet and fill the syringe.

"We don't feed you here," Edwards said. "You feed yourself. You've got to start using your hands sometime." He waited while the medic searched for a place to give the injection. "In his arm," he said.

The corpsman found a small, unburnt area near the elbow and plunged the needle into the skin. David, watching him, visibly relaxed. He turned his head on the board and looked at Edwards.

"We can help you grow new skin, stop your infections, graft you—if it comes to that. But it will all be for nothing if you leave here with all your joints tied down by scar tissue. If you don't exercise and keep the scar tissue and new skin over your joints loose and flexible it will tie 'em down like iron. All that new skin and scar that will be forming has a tendency to contract with time. If you don't keep it loose, you'll leave here as much a cripple as if someone had shot off your arms and legs. Your hands aren't that bad, David. We'll start today with them."

"But I can't hold a fork."

"We'll put wooden blocks on them, and as you get used to handling one size, we'll make the blocks smaller. Understood?"

"Yes, sir."

"You married, David?" Edwards asked.

"No."

The corpsman, pulling off a piece of skin, left an area red and oozing. David, stretched out and relaxed in the water, his head bobbing a bit, didn't even notice.

"Engaged?"

"Yes, sir."

"Would you like me to write her for you?"

David closed his eyes. "No, sir, I don't think so."

"All right. I'll check on you later."

When he got back to the office he found Johnson working at his desk.

"Coffee?" Johnson asked.

"No, thanks."

"We're getting three more today. Colonel Volpe called. Apparently you said you'd be too busy to take two VIP's around."

"That's right, I'm no goddam press agent. You show 'em around."

That evening, despite the fact that Johnson was on call, Edwards went back to the ward. All the patients had been settled in for the night. The ward master was in the treatment room, cutting adhesive tape into twelve-inch strips.

"What's new, White?"

"Nothing, Doc, really. Same old thing."

"How's Jensen doing?"

White put his scissors back into his pocket. "He's doing all right. We drew two blood cultures on him this evening and sent a titer off for moniliasis. He had some difficulty using the blocks, but he got a few bites down; seems as if the sulfamyelon is bothering him—stinging him. You never know who it's going to bother."

277

"And the three new ones?"

"They're OK," White said. "Hardly burned at all. Don't even know why they came here."

"It's the Army's idea," Edwards said, and giving him a parting pat, walked out into the unit. David was on a Stryker frame halfway down the ward, lying on his stomach. White sulfamyelon cream was smeared all over his burned back, buttocks, and legs.

"How's it going?"

"Fine, sir."

"The ward master told me that you did all right at supper."

"Yes, sir."

Later that evening, one of David's blood cultures began to grow out Pseudomonas arinosa. The bacteriology lab called the ward, and the ward master called Edwards. He told the ward master to restart David's IV and put him of 200 mg of polymyxin every four hours.

The next morning, after rounds, Johnson got him alone. "About Jensen's polymyxin," he said. "Do you think his kidneys are good enough to handle that big dose?"

"What would you suggest?" Edwards asked.

"You could destroy his kidneys with that much poly-myxin."

"I could save him too."

"If he's going to die," Johnson said, "he's going to die. He's 80-percent burned, and his blood culture is already growing out pseudomonas."

"I know. That's the great thing I learned from my trip back to America. His death is expected. It is expected since there are 80 percent burns, and it is expected that

80 percent will become septic. The whole thing is expected. You're supposed to get burned in Nam; you're supposed to get your legs blown off; you're supposed to get your chopper shot down; you're supposed to get killed. It's just not something that happens. It's expected."

When Edwards came back to the ward, he found David lying on his back, and the corpsman was smearing on the last of the sulfamyelon, spreading it over David's charred stomach as if it were butter.

"This stuff stings, honest, Doc," David said. "It just keeps stinging."

"I know," Edwards said. "It does that sometimes, but it will get better with time. You sort of build up a tolerance to it. The point is that you need it now. It keeps your skin from getting infected and gives the new skin a chance to grow. Believe it or not, sulfamyelon is one of the major breakthroughs in the treatment of burns."

"Can't I have something for the stinging?"

"No, David, I'm sorry."

That evening, down in the hospital bacteriology lab, his second blood culture started growing out another patch of pure Pseudomonas.

When Edwards came to work up the new admissions the next day, he stopped by to see David. Unable to lift his head, he was fitted with prismatic lenses so he could see around him without having to lift his head. Someone had hooked a book rack onto the frame, but there was nothing on it. He was just lying there with the glasses on, staring at the ceiling.

"I asked the therapist for a mirror today," he said before Edwards had a chance to say hello.

"What did she say?"

"She didn't say anything."

"This is not the time for mirrors," Edwards said. "When things start healing up, I'll get you one. Don't worry, David, we've had guys here a lot worse off than you. They all healed. It took a while, but they did."

That afternoon they got in two more burns from Nam. One was from Laos. At least that's what the soldier said; his records read Vietnam.

In the evening, Edwards brought David a book. He found him on his stomach again, and he put the book on the night table next to the frame.

"How does the skin grow back?" David asked, speaking to the floor. The day before he had mentioned that there were sixteen different colors in the floor tiles. "I mean, where's it gonna come from?"

"From you."

"Yeah?" David said. "How?"

Edwards pulled up a chair. "You have enough, you don't really need very much," he explained. "The skin grows back from the areas around the hair follicles; the follicles go down pretty deep, down into the area below the skin. Below the burns the new skin grows out from the lining of these follicles, like grass out of a valley. These linings are like nature's reserves. The new skin just keeps growing out from them, creeping over the burned area, until all these little growing areas come together."

"Why am I going to have to be grafted then?" David asked sullenly.

Edwards sensed the despair in his question. "Some-

280

times," he said, trying to sound reasonable, "if the burns are too deep, deep enough to destroy the follicles, then there is no skin to grow back, so we have to graft."

"Where are you going to get the skin for that?"

"From your friends, David," Edwards said gently, "from your friends."

The morning culture again grew out Pseudomonas. That afternoon they took David to the operating room and covered his legs and part of his stomach with cadaver skin. When Edwards visited him again that evening, he complained that his head hurt and that the sulfamyelon was stinging even more.

"What will you do when you get home?" Edwards asked.

David was sullen. "School, I guess."

"You've got to be more positive than that," Edwards said coaxingly.

"I was positive before I got burned."

"I'm telling you, you're going to be OK."

"I didn't even see it," David said reproachfully. "I was just walking. I wasn't even point. I swear to God, I didn't even hear it. Can you believe that?" he said loudly. "I couldn't even goddamn hear it."

Within three days the cadaver grafts failed, refused to take, and Edwards had to order it pulled off, like the rest of the dying skin. David, lying in the water, saw him as soon as he walked into the treatment room.

"I'm handling it, dammit," he said belligerently. "Just leave me alone, will you? Just goddamn leave me alone."

That evening David ignored his presence.

"I saw you with some letters this afternoon," Edwards

said, noting that the whitish scar tissue under David's chin had a pale greenish cast to it. "Nice handwriting. Your girl?"

"No, my family."

"What did they say?"

"It's in the drawer."

Edwards opened the drawer of the nightstand next to the frame. It was a rather bright letter, careful, measuredly written, filled with support and concern. There was a section about Carol, how much she loved David and how happy she was that he was finally out of the fighting.

"Did you answer?" Edwards asked.

"I didn't know how."

"They know you're burned," Edwards refolded the letter. "It seems to me they're holding up quite well. The least you could do is help them out."

David slowly turned his head. His eyes, hollow holes, stared coldly and defiantly at Edwards. "I've been throwing up all day. I can't keep anything down."

"Yes," Edwards said calmly, putting the letter back in the drawer. "I know."

"I'm not going to make it, am I? No, no, don't interrupt. I know I'm not. That stuff you keep putting into my IV bottle—the only other guys who get it are the ones on respirators. I know," he said, almost triumphantly. "I've checked on the way to the whirlpool. I know." It was all there in his eyes—the pain, the suffering, the loss of belief.

It caught Edwards off guard. "I told you about the pain, didn't I?" he said angrily. "Have I bull-shitted you yet? Look, if you were going to die, I'd let you know. Right? I'd give you the chance to tie things up, understand?" A certain distance entered David's stare, a vague confusion that was more pathetic than his glaring hopelessness.

Edwards got up. "Now, dammit," he said, "I want you to think of an answer to that letter. I'll be back in the morning, and I want an answer. Is that clear?"

Depressed and angry, he left the ward. Outside he passed groups of patients from the other wards, some standing around talking, others doing nothing, or being pushed around in wheelchairs by their buddies. Johnson was right, he thought. David would die. He was probably, all things considered, dead the moment the round hit the rucksack.

Edwards went back to his room and sat there on the edge of his bed. There was really nothing left to do. Almost unconsciously he got up and walked wearily over to his desk, pulled open a drawer, and took out a folder that contained a passage he had once read. It had struck him so forcibly at the time that he had made a Xerox copy of it.

The dying experience is extremely traumatic to the young adult, to his family and the treating staff. The meaning of dying is appreciated by the young adult, but the reality of personal death is not accepted. He lusts for life, he now has the full emotional capability to sense the personal depth of meaning in death. As he strives for self-sufficiency and for independence, he can appreciate clearly the total passivity and the absolute dependency of the dying experience. In the solitude of death, the young child or the mature adult can turn to another for comfort without feeling childish or dependent. The newly emancipated, self-sufficient young adult may have too much personal pride to allow himself to accept the support and the understanding he so desperately needs as he moves toward death. The specific emotional reaction of the newly mature young man to the prospect of personal death is RAGE. He feels that life is completely within his grasp so that death above all else is the great ravisher and destroyer. These mature young men who have worked, trained and striven to reach self-confidence and self-sufficiency now appreciate what they can do and what they can enjoy and that suddenly it will all end. They are so ready to live, to them death is a brutal, personal attack, an unforgivable insult, a totally unacceptable event. The intensity of his natural understandable rage at this process of dying may cause an accentuation of physical pain. Normal bitterness may be expressed by lack of cooperation or even by open antagonism. The dying young adult may alienate himself from his family. If the physician and the treatment staff can understand this natural rage that they see in the young adult about to die, they may be able to help him cope with his emotional reaction in a fashion that does not disrupt the necessary treatment. The young physician himself responds with the normal rage reaction of the young dying adult. He sees death as a destroyer that must be fought with every means possible. This normal, youthful rage may lead the physician to assault the dying patient with all kinds of treatment procedures in an attempt to keep death away. The task of the physician is not to comprehend the incomprehensible, but to make the natural work of death and the mourning the most meaningful and most productive for the people with which he deals.

The phone woke him a little past three in the morning. "Major!"

"Yeah." Edwards fumbled across the night table for the lamp switch.

"This is Sergeant Cramer. Jensen's temperature just spiked to 105."

"OK," Edwards said, switching on the light and sitting up. He cleared his throat. "I'll be right over." Even as he was hanging up, he was reaching under the bed for his shoes.

The ward master met him at the entrance to the unit and followed him hurriedly down the ward.

"He's becoming disoriented."

"What about the cultures?" Edwards asked quickly. "Still Pseudomonas?"

"No, this morning's grew out Klebsiella."

David was lying on the frame. All the covers were off, and he was trembling.

"106," the medic said, reading the stool-smeared thermometer.

"Better add some kanamycin and Keflin to the chloromycetin. How's the blood pressure?"

"Stable."

"How much kanamycin and Keflin?" Cramer asked.

"A lot, a lot. Just get it!"

Cramer looked at him and quickly left to get the antibiotics.

"David, David," Edwards leaned over the frame. "David!"

Slowly he opened his eyes, but there was no light in them, no gleam.

"Listen," Edwards said, lowering his voice. "I'm going to have to put you on a cooling blanket; it's not going to be comfortable, but your temperature . . ."

"I can't think of anything," David said, closing his eyes again.

"He's been confused for the last hour," the medic said.

A moment later, the ward master came back with the

antibiotics already drawn up into two syringes. While he shot the drugs directly into the IV bottle, Edwards said, "We'd better put in a central venous pressure. How's his urine output?"

"Down 60 cc in the last two hours."

"Does he have any blood cross-matched?"

"Four units."

"Respirator?"

"There's one down in central supply. We can get it any time."

"What about his monalisis titers?"

"Still normal."

"White count?"

"The lab technicians are doing it now."

"Let's see his electrolytes."

"Doc."

Surprised, Edwards turned around. David had stopped shivering.

"Doc!"

Edwards hurriedly bent over the frame.

David stared up at him, his eyes strangely clear and deep. "You didn't have to come, not all the time."

"I wanted to," Edwards said.

"They told me about your brother and your taking him home." David was about to go on when, gasping, he suddenly bolted upright and, struggling against the restraints, vomited up a great flood of bright red blood.

Dying in the burn unit is not normally that dramatic. There is usually very little blood; burns die inside out, down at the cellular level, where the billions of struggling cells just simply give up. It is for the most part a kind of gentle going; breathing becomes labored and distant, circulation falls apart, hearts dilate, livers and spleens grow to twice their size, lungs gradually fill with fluid, and there is always a certain period of confusion. But after it, a comfortable time of unconsciousness, where nothing is done and everything—even the last breath— is a rather leisurely giving up.

Suddenly, with the blood still welling out of his lipless mouth, David went rigid and, arching backwards, collapsed against the frame. Edwards grabbed the suction off the wall and, pulling open David's jaw, began sucking out his mouth, trying to clear the blood and vomit out of his airway. The gasping stopped and there was the more comfortable sound of air moving in and out.

"Get the blood," Edwards ordered, reaching for the oxygen mask. He was turning up the oxygen flow just as Cramer came running back with the blood.

"Call Johnson. Set up a cut-down tray and get a tracheotomy set."

The ward master unhooked the IV from its bottles. "The blood is still ice cold," he said.

"Just hang it," Edwards ordered, holding open David's jaw, trying to get out more of the blood. "Just goddamn hang it. And call the general surgeon . . . David! David!" He pressed the oxygen mask over the boy's mouth and he could feel the new skin slipping away under the pressure of the mask's rubber edges. "David! David! Can you hear me? OK, listen, you have a stress ulcer. We might have to operate tonight. You have a lot of blood and stuff in your lungs. I'm going to have to put you on a respirator. It will help you breathe, so I'll have to make a little hole in your windpipe. It won't hurt." He looked up, checking the blood running down into the IV tubing. "It's just to help you breathe. Honest. Just to breathe."

The corpsman had set up the tracheotomy, and Edwards held the oxygen mask in place while the ward master quickly cleaned David's neck as best he could. The noise coming from inside the lungs was getting louder again. Even with the oxygen David was having to fight to breathe.

"I'm going to make the hole now," Edwards said, removing the mask. Little bits of skin came away with it.

"Doc," David gasped. "Take me home, too . . . please, Doc . . . I don't want to go home alone."

GLOSSARY OF MILITARY

AND MEDICAL TERMS

AK-47   Communist 7.62-mm semi-automatic and fully automatic assault rifle.

AK-50   The newest version of an AK-47. Some have a permanently mounted "illegal" triangular bayonet, which leaves a sucking wound that will not close.

Angel track   An APC used as an aid station.

AOD   Administrative officer on duty.

APC   Armored personnel carrier.

APL   Barrack ship.

AR   Army Regulation.

ARVN   Army Republic of Vietnam.

Bandoliers   Belts of machine-gun ammunition.

Big Boys   Slang for tanks.

Boonies   The countryside.

Bouncing Betty   A mine with two charges: one to propel the explosive charge upward and the other set to explode at about waist level.

Bravo   Army designation for the infantry man.

Burr Holes   Surgical holes drilled through the skull so that the brain and its surrounding vessels can be operated on.

CA   Combat assault. Term applied to taking troopers into a hot landing zone.

C and C Chopper   Command and control. The helicopter the unit commander rides and from which he directs the battle.

Camies   World War II term for camouflage uniforms.

Chicom Mine   A Chinese Communist mine. It can be made of plastic.

Chopper   Helicopter.

Claymores   Anti-personnel mines containing thousands of little steel balls that blow outward, covering an arch of about 120 degrees.

Cobra   Heavily armed assault helicopter.

CP   Command post.

CP Pills   Anti-malarial pills.

DEROS   Date of Estimated Return from overseas.

Dust Off   Medical evacuation mission by helicopter. The term refers to the great amount of dust thrown up by the rotors as the med evacs come in to land.

Enucleation   Surgical removal of the eye.

ENT   Ear, nose, and throat.

EOD   Explosive ordinance disposal.

FDC   Fire-direction control center.

Fifty-one (51)   Heavy Communist machine gun.

Fire Base   An artillery battery set up to give fire support to surrounding units.

Fire Track   Flame-thrower tank.

FO   Forward observer.

Fours (4's)   F-4 Phantom jet fighter bombers.

Grids   A map broken into numbered thousand-meter squares.

Grunt   Originally slang for a Marine fighting in Vietnam, but later applied to any soldier fighting there.

HALO   High-altitude, low-opening jumping for insertion of troops behind enemy lines. The jump is begun from 15,000 feet, with an average free-fall time of approximately seventeen minutes.

H and E   High explosive.

Horn   Radio microphone.

ICU   Intensive-care unit.

Intubate   To thread a hollow tube down into the windpipe to facilitate breathing.

IV   Intravenous injection.

KIA   Killed in action.

Lager   A night defensive perimeter.

Laparotomy   Surgical exploration of the abdomen.

Lego   Infantry unit.

LOH (pronounced "loach")   Light observation helicopter.

Glossary of Military and Medical Terms

LRRP   Long-range reconnaisance patrol. Now called LRP (long-range patrol). Initially four- or five-man teams that would go out for recon; now ten- to twenty-man ambush patrols.

LST   Landing ship tank.

L, V, X   Different types of ambush setups.

LZ   Landing zone.

M-16   American 5.56-mm infantry rifle.

M-60   American 7.62-mm machine gun.

MACV   Military Assistance Command Vietnam.

Med Cap   Medical civil assistance program for Vietnamese civilians.

MOS   Military occupational specialty.

Moose   Mistress

NCO   Noncommissioned officer.

Nephrectomy   Surgical removal of a kidney.

NPD   Night perimeter defense.

NVA   North Vietnamese Army.

OR   Operating room.

Point   The lead man in a patrol.

Pseudomonas   Bacillus resistant to most antibiotics.

Recondo School   A training school in country (Vietnam) to train LRRP's. The largest is at Na Trang, where the training action is taken against the 17th NVA Division.

Red Legs   Slang for Artillery. In the Civil War Union Artillery men had red stripes on their pants.

RPD   A 7.62-mm Communist machine gun with a 100-round, belt-operated drum that fires the same round as the AK-47.

RPG   A Communist self-propelled rocket.

RTO   Radio telephone operator.

S-2   Designation of intelligence staff for a unit.

S-5   Designation of civic staff officer for a unit.

Salvo   Firing a battery in unison.

SF   Special Forces.

SI   Seriously ill.

Slick   Helicopter for transporting troops.

SOP   Standard operating practice or procedure.

Stryker Frames   Hospital beds set up so that a patient placed between two large metal arches can be easily turned over.

TAC   Tactical air strikes.

Tango Boat   Armored landing craft mounted with 50-caliber machine guns; also 40-caliber anti-aircraft gun used for direct fire.

Thorazine   A tranquilizer.

Tiger Suits   Camouflage fatigue uniforms.

Titers   Amount of anti-body in serum.

TOC   Tactical operation center, usually battalion level and above.

Track   Any vehicle that moves on treads instead of wheels.

Triage   The sorting out of patients according to the criticalness of their needs, i.e., those who need immediate surgery versus those who need only minimal care.

USARV   United States Army Republic Vietnam.

VC   Viet Cong.

Vena Cava   The large vein draining blood back to the heart, the superior vena cava draining the whole upper half of the body, and the interior vena cava draining the lower extremities and trunk.

Ventricular Shunts   Tubes, surgically placed, which drain excessive fluid from the ventricles of the brain.

VSI   Very seriously ill. Army designation for those troopers who may die without immediate and definitive medical care.

WP   White phosphorous.